Big God
in a Little City

Todd Hudnall

insight publishing group

Tulsa, Oklahoma

BIG GOD IN A LITTLE CITY

Big God in a Little City by Todd Hudnall
Published by Insight Publishing Group
8801 S. Yale, Suite 410
Tulsa, OK 74137
918-493-1718

Unless otherwise noted all Scripture quotations are quoted from the New King James version of the Bible. Copyright © 1979, 1980, 1982 by Thomas Nelson, Inc., publishers.

ISBN 1-930027-45-1
Library of Congress catalog card number: 2001095954

Printed in the United States of America

TABLE OF CONTENTS

FOREWORD BY TOMMY BARNETT
ACKNOWLEDGMENTS
ENDORSEMENTS
PREFACE

Chapter 1 - PREPARATION   15
      Key 1 - Allow God to Prepare You

Chapter 2 - CALLING   21
      Key 2 - Hear the Call of God

Chapter 3 - LEADERSHIP   29
      Key 3 - Be a Servant Leader
      Key 4 - You Must First Lead Yourself

Chapter 4 - STRATEGIC PLANNING   43
      Key 5 - Receive a Vision from God
      Key 6 - Invest Time and Effort into
              Strategic Planning

Chapter 5 - HEALTHY MINISTRY   55
      Key 7 - Be a Healthy Person
      Key 8 - Be Real, Be Relevant, and Have Fun
      Key 9 - Work Hard
      Key 10 - Learn from Others
      Key 11 - Keep the Church in Balance

Chapter 6 - OUTREACH   65
    Key 12 - Be Outreach Focused

Chapter 7 - CHURCH GROWTH   79
    Key 13 - Intentionally Assimilate Newcomers
    Key 14 - Prepare for Growth

Chapter 8 - PRAYER   91
    Key 15 - Become a House of Prayer

Chapter 9 - MINISTRY   99
    Key 16 - Equip and Release the Laity
    Key 17 - Small Groups Make a Big Difference
    Key 18 - Invest in Leaders

Chapter 10 - HIDDEN KEYS   107
    Key 19 - Hire Staff from Within
    Key 20 - Invest in Children and Teenagers
    Key 21 - Get Involved in What God Is Doing
    Key 22 - Have a World Vision
    Key 23 - Keep Getting Better
    Key 24 - Break Through Barriers with
            Prayer and Fasting
    Key 25 - Stay Long Enough to Make a Difference

APPENDIX
ENDNOTES

FOREWORD

The title of this book suggests its usefulness. There are many books written on how to grow churches in great metropolitan areas, but the dynamics of church growth in a small community are different. It is important to note that while the dynamics are different, the principles are similar.

Therefore, I am excited to endorse the work of this great pastor; our principals are similar. This church has impacted its community in a manner which is, in many ways, greater than the impact of a large church in a major city.

Equally important is the humble approach of expressing ideas that have worked, and encouraging each pastor to get their own vision from God for their maximum impact in their won community. Of special note are the chapters on "Healthy Ministry" and "Hidden Keys".

Everyone who reads this book will be inspired and encouraged to do their very best for God, and that is a wonderful testimony to this great work in Lufkin, Texas.

Tommy Barnett
Senior Pastor
First Assembly of God
Phoenix, Arizona

ACKNOWLEDGEMENTS

I want to thank the gracious, generous, and faithful people of First Assembly of God in Lufkin, Texas. Your fervent passion for God and sacrificial dedication to the cause of Christ inspire me. You are some of the greatest people in the world.

ENDORSEMENTS

Many a pastor has prayed and worked for church growth in relatively small towns across America with little measurable results. First Assembly of God in Lufkin, Texas, was just such a church—a good church with good pastors that had remained status quo for a number of years.

In 1991, Todd and Kelly Hudnall arrived in Lufkin and ten years of meteoric soul-winning growth began for First Assembly. *Big God in a Little City* is the story of this marvelous growth. You will be blessed and inspired by this account of God in action in the lives of dedicated people.

Derwood W. Dubose
District Superintendent
North Texas District of the Assemblies of God

❏ ❏ ❏

Big God in a Little City is long overdue. It is proof that smaller communities can give birth to larger, dynamic churches. Todd Hudnall has effectively combined the supernatural components and the pragmatic keys necessary for a healthy church.

I believe every minister in the Arkansas District Council of the Assemblies of God could benefit from Todd's insight, instruction, and example. Many of our churches are in rural areas, and I am sure this book will be a textbook of encouragement.

Alton Garrison, D.D.
District Superintendent
Arkansas District Council of the Assemblies of God

□ □ □

What an enjoyable book to read. *Big God in a Little City* is the story of how Todd Hudnall went to First Assembly of God in Lufkin, Texas, in 1991, when the church had an average attendance of 250 per Sunday and only thirty conversions in the previous year. Now they are averaging 1500 and 1199 conversions in the last year. This book describes the reasons why this church exploded in growth even though it was in small town. However, the reader will not just see and hear great stories, Hudnall examines the causes back of the growth; and he puts these into principles so that other churches in small towns can apply the same techniques. Therefore as you read, there are numerous stories to keep you interested, yet there's always the explanation to help you understand.

Perhaps the best contributions are the appendices at the back of the book that include the personal core values and the mission statement of Todd Hudnall. Every pastor should read these and write his own. Then the core values and mission statement of First Assembly are included along with a vision statement. Every church in a small town should follow this example and write their core values and mission statements; and in the discipline of writing what they believe and where they are going; they have also begun to take the journey of building a church in a small town.

Elmer L. Towns
Author and Dean of School of Religion
Liberty University
Lynchburg, Virginia

❏ ❏ ❏

It's absolutely amazing to see what God has accomplished through Todd and Kelly in small town U.S.A. They have developed the keys to move us past thoughts of revival into the realities of revolution! The following pages are the results of a Big God living, moving and directing small human minds into visual effectiveness. More than a story, this book is a gift of faith that will ignite your passion and transform your vision into a radical, authentic dream. God bless you, Todd, for your contribution to all us little guys who haven't given up yet.

Pastor Roosevelt Hunter
First Assembly of God
Holland, Michigan

PREFACE

There is no club, group, society, institution, or organization that compares to the Church of Jesus Christ. When the Church functions according to the Biblical pattern, it is indeed glorious. It is the pearl of great price, Christ's own body, which the Lord purchased with His own blood and that He is building into His prevailing and beautiful bride.

When I was a young believer, sensing a call into the ministry, I was captured with the dream of being part of such a church—a church that corporately lived the life of Jesus, transformed its community, and impacted the world with the powerful gospel of God's grace. I would sit silently in the dark, tears streaming down my face, as I pondered what it would be like to pastor such a church.

This book is the story of my experience as the senior pastor of First Assembly of God in Lufkin, Texas. Though I am not satisfied that I've been a part of all Jesus intends for His Church, I have been part of the fulfillment of a dream: the dream of broken hearts being healed, marriages being reconciled, individual lives being transformed, a community being impacted and God being glorified through His people. This is not a blueprint for building a model church; rather, I hope to share with other pastors the experiences I have had and the lessons I have learned that may assist them in cooperating with God in pastoring a church that makes a difference. Over the years I've read many quality books on effective church ministry. Mega-church pastors in major metropolitan areas have written the majority of these books. Interestingly, I have never seen a book on growing an effective church written by a pastor from a small population area. This book is an attempt to fill that void and to share many of the experiences we've had, the principles we've learned, and the strategies we've attempted at First Assembly of God in Lufkin, Texas (population 34,000). It is the story of the work of a big God in a little city.

During my nine-and-a-half years at First Assembly, the church has grown from a congregation of 250, to a vibrant, dynamic, life-producing body of believers currently averaging 1,600 in Sunday morning worship. We've seen over 6,000 documented salvation experiences; participated in the healing of hundreds of lives and marriages; and witnessed miraculous deliverances from addictions, bondages, and the powers of darkness. This inwardly focused, plateaued, white, aging, and divided congregation of 250 has become a healthy, vibrant, multi-generational, racially diverse church, profoundly impacting our region with the gospel of the Lord Jesus Christ. There are many churches in America that desperately need this same kind of metamorphosis. God has done great things at First Assembly. He wants to do the same and more for every church that is willing to recognize its need for His touch and will cry out to Him to become a difference-maker in its community.

Over the years I've had numerous people ask me, "What has been the key to the growth and effectiveness of your church?" I initially tried to answer that question until I came to realize there was no single key. In Matthew 16:19 Jesus said, "And I will give you the keys of the kingdom of heaven." Notice that there is no single key to the kingdom. Neither is there a *single* key to why a church experiences sustained health and growth. I've identified twenty-five different keys to our success. I will attempt to share with you those keys and how they have been worked out in my life and at First Assembly of God in Lufkin, Texas.

Chapter 1

PREPARATION

Key One
Allow God to Prepare You

> *But now,* O LORD, *you are our Father;*
> *we are the clay, and You our potter;*
> *and all we are the work of Your hand.*
> Isaiah 64:8

Preparation always precedes usefulness. God is always preparing us for the next adventure in our lives. The greater the plan the more preparation is required. Few are those who immediately explode into ministry usefulness and effectiveness. Those who do often fade out as quickly as they entered. God's way to fruitfulness requires preparation. Ask Moses who spent forty years in the desert wasteland before becoming Israel's deliverer, or Joseph who spent thirteen years in Egyptian incarceration before becoming its prime minister, or Jesus who was thirty years old before beginning his earthly ministry. Part of that preparation involves prayer, study, and service; but it may also involve "the dark night of the soul," in which God shapes us for His purposes. I've become a big proponent of formal education for pastoral training, but the preparation that has meant the most in my life did not come from the halls of higher learning. Rather, it came from the crucible of my first pastoral assignment.

First Assembly in Lufkin is not the first church I have pastored. In 1984, I pioneered an independent Charismatic church in Topeka, Kansas. I was a relatively new Christian with no Bible college education or seminary training and no significant ministry experience, but I did have a passion for God and a desire to build a great church. I was single at the time and moved to Topeka along with two friends, whom I had inspired with the vision and who wanted to help me in the work. Within a year and a half, the church had grown to 170 in Sunday morning worship attendance. That is when my inexperience, lack of knowledge, insecurities, and spiritual immaturity caught up with me. It wasn't any single incident but a series of poor leadership choices that cost us our momentum and led to a two-year slide in attendance and offerings.

During this period of the implosion of that church, a number of other personal setbacks and heartbreaks also occurred. It eventually led me to a time of despair, discouragement, depression, and mental torment. In behavior, I was living an exemplary Christian life. I was a diligent pastor, living a holy life and spending several hours in the Scripture and in prayer daily. I sought counsel from various friends and ministers but no one had any answers for me. A couple of the counselors assumed I must have some secret hidden sin in my life. They were wrong. I had to seek out additional counsel because it seemed most of my ministry friends had forsaken me. My small congregation was encouraging and loving toward me, but I didn't feel I should confide in any of them. After a few months, I decided not to trouble anyone else and I kept my misery to myself. I reached a time of deep self-hatred and agonizing hopelessness. The Lord was my One constant companion. Though I talked and cried out to Him continually, it seemed He wasn't listening. I felt that He loved me and cared about me but saw me as an impossible case.

By various means, during the fall of 1988, the Holy Spirit began dealing with me about unconditional surrender. He targeted a particular area of my life. I was a twenty-nine-year-old bachelor. Getting married had never been a priority in my life; I simply assumed that when I needed to get married, God would bring the right person. I was content as a bachelor, with my primary focus being the call of God on my life.

I finally met and dated someone I thought I could marry; however, with time we realized it wasn't the will of God. Due to situations surrounding the breakup and the absence of other close friends at the same time, I experienced a new loneliness and sense of emptiness in my life. Suddenly I had it in my head that marriage was the greatest need of my life.

I'm embarrassed now to admit that it had become an obsession for me. Daily I spent a good deal of time in prayer for a wife. In addition I spent much of my idle time thinking about it or casually talking to the Lord about it. I'd even written out a list of nine qualities I was looking for in a mate. I prayed over the list every day. Yet, during that year I didn't meet any Christian women that interested me.

In retrospect, I now see that marriage at that point in my life would have been the worst possible thing for me. I thought I could find in a wife what could only be found in God. There were probably many issues in my life, but the Lord zeroed in on that specific area. I knew I had to give this desire over to Him.

There was a real sense that in giving it to the Lord, I would likely remain celibate the rest of my life. I didn't want celibacy. In my mind marriage equaled companionship, greater ministry success, happiness, and fulfillment. For three days I battled with this issue and the bigger issue of total, unconditional surrender of every area of my life.

Over those days I became increasingly weak and restless. Finally the moment of surrender came. Standing beside the microwave oven of my apartment, I came to the end of my stubborn rebellion. I said, "Lord, I give up on all of my dreams. I don't care whether I ever get married. I don't care what becomes of my life. All I want is You. I completely give my life to you."

At that very moment, something quite amazing happened to me. I was filled with a revelation of Jesus Christ as "my everything." Instantly every bit of depression, discouragement, defeat, fear, worry, insecurity, rejection, and condemnation left me. In its place were love, joy, hope, confidence, and the most outrageous peace you could ever imagine. I sensed no unique physical manifestation, only an internal release of the darkness and a flooding of my soul with light.

It was as if I met Jesus face to face. Suddenly He was truly Lord, He was truly in control, and He was truly all that I needed. During the next few days, I lived in a state of heavenly bliss. Nothing bothered me, concerned me, or enticed me. Jesus Christ was all that mattered, all I wanted to think about, all I wanted to talk about, and all that I wanted to live for. I cannot possibly explain the indescribable state of wholeness and completeness in Christ. After a few days, I came back to the realities of life, but my life was touched by God in a way that would never leave me the same.

Since this painful yet glorious experience, I've come to see how necessary it was. Reading about the lives of other Christians and observing the lives of other believers, I've come to the realization that before someone can be greatly used of God, they must be greatly broken by God. From

Abraham at Mount Moriah offering Issac, to Moses tending sheep as an escaped fugitive from Egypt, to David fleeing from King Saul, to the apostle Paul struggling with a thorn in the flesh, it is imperative that there come a time when our dependence upon the flesh is broken and we surrender all to God.

Shortly after this encounter with God, I went on a ministry trip with Greg Varney, a pastor friend of mine in the city. On the way home from our trip, we somehow began to discuss the possibility of merging our church bodies. In January of 1989, the churches were merged into one body called Light of the World Christian Center. I became the associate pastor of the church. Through the process Greg was very generous to me and gracious in receiving the members of the church I formerly pastored.

His leadership made it work, but from the beginning the Lord told me, "If this marriage of churches fails to succeed, it will be because you fail to be a servant." That strong warning helped make the merger a wonderful success. The merger brought a new synergy and momentum that propelled the church forward. Light of the World Christian Center is currently a thriving outreach-oriented church making a difference in Topeka, Kansas.

Chapter 2

CALLING

Key Two
Hear the Call of God

*Now after he had seen the vision, immediately we
sought to go to Macedonia, concluding that the Lord
had called us to preach the gospel to them.*
Acts16:10

During my ministry at First Assembly, I have been
presented with opportunities to go to other churches. Most
of the time, accepting such an offer seemed to be in my best
interest, but it was easy to stay because I knew God had
called Kelly and me to our church. This doesn't mean I
would never leave where I am, but it does mean I would not
leave my sure calling in Lufkin unless I was confident about
a new calling. That sense of calling will keep you going when
you feel like giving up. I'd like to relate to you the story of
the calling Kelly and I received to First Assembly. It's the call
that almost wasn't.

After a year on staff at Light of the World, the church
helped me launch out into traveling ministry, as I served as
an evangelist sent out by the church. During that time I met
my wife, Kelly, and we were married in the spring of 1991.
Now that I no longer saw marriage as a great need in my life,
and I had learned to find fulfillment in Christ, it was safe for
me to get married. Interestingly Kelly met all of the qualifi-
cations on my "dream girl" list. It included a passion for

Christ and a call to ministry. My time on staff at Light of the World was a healing season full of wonderful memories but in my heart still burned the desire to serve as a senior pastor once again.

Following our wedding, Kelly and I began to pray about where the Lord would have us pastor. Due to a desire for accountability and to be part of a larger organization, I had transferred my ministry credentials to the Assemblies of God. We contacted a few districts to ask for open church lists, yet we didn't want to go through the process the same way people hunt for a job. We were determined not to send out a stack of résumés in search of a good church. Instead, our desire was to wait for God to open His door. As such, we daily prayed in the Spirit and asked the Lord to work in our hearts through people and in our circumstances to reveal His will. I actually compiled a list of twelve characteristics I wanted in the church we would pastor.

One evening I received a call from a pastor whose church I had ministered in. He told me of an interesting opportunity in Lufkin, Texas. As he described the church, my heart began to race. It sounded strikingly like my list. Of course, I told Kelly about the church. She had never before heard of Lufkin, but that very night one of her customers at work mentioned that she was from Lufkin. Over the next couple of days, I could not get Lufkin, Texas, out of my mind. We felt this might be the place God was calling us, and we sent the church a résumé and information packet.

First Assembly of God in Lufkin had been founded in 1927. It had become a strong vibrant church in the late 1970s but had since plateaued in growth and in community influence. The church membership had experienced division and turmoil. A few years before, the long-term pastor of the church was voted out of office by the church membership, and some of the members followed him across town to found a new church.

During that time First Assembly lost its sovereignty, and the denomination appointed a new pastor to the church. The new pastor was able to return some stability to the church but left after two years with the body still in need of restoration and healing. First Assembly was looking for a mature pastor who had already raised a family and who had experienced success in his former pastorates. Obviously, this newlywed couple wasn't anything like their vision of what their pastor should be. As one pulpit committee member put it, we were "barely married and barely Assembly of God."

Out of the stack of dozens of résumés and cassette preaching tapes the committee was looking through, one of my messages aroused their interest. We were asked to come and minister at the church, if for no other reason than to fill the pulpit for a Sunday, but God had other ideas. After spending a couple days at the church, we knew it was where God wanted us. Following our first trip, the pulpit committee in a split vote decided to have us return to actually candidate and be voted on. We were so certain God had called us to Lufkin, we canceled the lease on our apartment and canceled all the engagements we were able to cancel.

This time our trip to Lufkin seemed even better. We had already developed some strong relationships with these people we had just gotten acquainted with. My Sunday morning message seemed to have a special heavenly empowerment on it, and a couple people responded to the call for salvation. I was told it was the first time they had seen people come to Christ in a church service in a very long time. Kelly and I were equally excited about the evening service.

Following the service the members were supposed to elect their new pastor. We left the sanctuary and went to the church's evangelist quarters, where we were staying. Following the election we planned to go out and celebrate with members of our new congregation. Their vote took longer than we expected. Finally, we heard a knock at the door. I was still in the back room as Kelly excitedly answered the door, expecting a hearty, "congratulations." Instead, she was greeted with tears as we were told that we didn't receive the 67 percent vote required; we were four votes short. At first, we thought it was a joke but quickly realized our new friends were serious. For the next twenty minutes, we sat in stunned silence, occasionally saying to each other, "I can't believe this" or "How is this possible?"

Finally I turned to Kelly and said, "This morning we were rejoicing and praising God for His goodness in bringing us to this church. Now that our dream is shattered, He is no less worthy of praise. We have to have a private praise service." We went together into the small and now empty sanctuary of the church and began to worship and praise God with all of our hearts. At first our worship was forced, but after a short time in His presence, we were glorifying the changeless God who was still in control and worthy of our worship.

After about thirty minutes of praising and worshiping the Lord, I became aware that we were not alone. Several people from the church had joined us and were praying throughout the sanctuary. A few minutes later, Kelly came to me and said, "Todd, I believe God has spoken to me and said it isn't over."

I said, "Honey face reality; it is over, but God has another plan for us." After about an hour of prayer, we spent some time visiting with and praying with some of the members who came to be with us. I thought it was our last good-bye, but God had other plans.

My mother is a woman of prayer who has often heard from the Lord through dreams. I'd already notified her of what had happened in Lufkin, and when we returned from Texas, I received a phone call from her. She had called Kelly and me the Sunday morning we were in Lufkin just prior to the morning service. That morning she related to me two dreams she had been given.

On July 24, 1991, I woke up. I'm not sure if I fell back to sleep or not, but I saw right in front of my face a blue paper. I could only see the writing on the very bottom of the page. On one straight line it said, "Congratulations Todd and Kelly." I knew the Lord was showing me something. I was certain it meant Todd and Kelly would be accepted as the new pastors of the church in Lufkin.

On August 4, 1991, early in the morning, I had a second dream. This was the same day that the church in Lufkin was voting on Todd as their new pastor. In my dream I saw the face of my mother. She was looking up and intensely interceding in prayer. In my dream I sensed many other people around, but I did not see their faces. All of the people and I had the feeling of discouragement and the feeling that things were not going to work out. It was a hopeless feeling.

This went on for quite some time, but then I saw a man whom I recognized. He also seemed discouraged and tired of all the struggle, but after a while he swung a whip in the air and proclaimed in a loud voice that the breakthrough had come, and everyone began to applaud and was happy. When I woke up I immediately felt it had something to do with Todd and the church he was a candidate for. I then thought it meant he would get the pastoral position, but I couldn't understand why there was all the discouragement about it.

My mother had related the dream to me early Sunday morning prior to the morning service. I thought it was an interesting dream, but I didn't give it much consideration. There was little doubt in my mind that we would be the new pastors of the church.

After returning home to Kansas my mother called and rehearsed the dream to me once again. She told me she felt the dream was directly referring to our situation. She felt my grandmother praying meant it was critical that the people of First Assembly should be seriously praying for God's will to be done in getting a pastor for their fellowship.

Out of genuine concern for the church, I called one of the members of the church we had gotten close to during our visit. I called to encourage her to have the church gather in prayer concerning their pastoral selection process, despite the fact that I no longer thought we were going to be their pastor.

Before I could say anything about it, she began to tell me about the wonderful prayer meetings the church had been having. The incident of the divided vote had led to a serious seeking after the heart of God. As they did, God began to move on their hearts. Individuals began to repent of their sins against God and toward one another. A few days later, the church called to tell me that the deacon board had accepted a petition to have a second vote on me as a pastoral candidate. They asked their sectional presbyter if that were permissible. He told them he had never heard of such a thing, but he saw nothing wrong with bringing it to another vote. A week later the church officially called to ask me to be their new pastor. Many of our friends thought we were crazy accepting the pastorate under such strange circumstances, but we were confident God was in it.

The first time we went to the church, there was a minister named B.A. Reeves who had retired from his pastorate several years before and was serving at First Assembly as a visitation and senior citizen's pastor. The first time we visited the church, he didn't think we could possibly be God's choice. We were too young and too inexperienced. After our visit, Reverend Reeves was up late at night praying. He cried out, "God, send the man you have for this church." He says that the Lord clearly spoke to him, saying, "I have sent the man." At that moment he knew we were God's choice for the church. Following all that had occurred, he related this story to me and to the church. This moving testimony from a person with the proven integrity of the godly Reverend Reeves gave many members of the church hope that God was up to something significant.

Our story is less spectacular than some are, and it is more dramatic that most tend to be. The principal to this key is not in the circumstances involving it but in knowing that you're called. There are many avenues God uses to confirm His calling in our lives. It certainly isn't a science, but I believe you can know when you have heard the call of God. I admonish pastors never to leave where they know God has assigned them until they are certain of a fresh calling to a new location.

Chapter 3

LEADERSHIP

Key Three
Be a Servant Leader

And He Himself gave some to be...pastors...
Ephesians 4:11

Jesus Christ calls some of His followers to be pastors, and He gives them to His Church. A pastor is a shepherd of God's people who is called to lead, feed, care, correct, and protect the flock of individuals God has entrusted to him. For a church to be a difference maker in its community, the senior pastor needs to develop his skills as a leader.

There is a great need for genuine pastoral leadership in the Church. "Social strategists see it. Church analysts note the same. There is a glut of the notable and notorious in every human arena, but too few leaders of substance and trust—too few by far to shape cities and congregations, let alone a nation or nations."[1]

A popular definition for leadership is "influence." For our purposes, pastoral leadership needs a broader definition than simply "influencing others." Christian leadership, and particularly pastoral leadership, has both a spiritual nature and a Godly character. Kenneth Gangel says, "We might describe Christian leadership as the exercise of one's spiritual gifts under the call of God to serve a certain group of people in achieving the goals God has given them toward the end of glorifying Christ."[2]

Another excellent definition comes from George Barna who defines a Christian leader as, "Someone who is called by God to lead and possess virtuous character and effectively motivates, mobilizes resources, and directs people toward the fulfillment of a jointly embraced vision from God."[3] Pastoral leadership goes beyond techniques and competencies to the heart of God being formed within the leader. When God came among men in the person of Jesus, He was a servant.

> *But Jesus called them to Himself and said to them, "You know that those who are considered rulers over the Gentiles lord it over them, and their great ones exercise authority over them. Yet it shall not be so among you; but whoever desires to become great among you shall be your servant. And whoever of you desires to be first shall be slave of all. For even the Son of Man did not come to be served, but to serve, and to give His life a ransom for many."*
>
> Mark 10:42-45

God has gifted and empowered all of His followers to be servants. The greatest in Christ's Kingdom are those who most obediently answer this call to servanthood. A leader in the church is not the one who has all the perks and privileges of being on top. Rather, in God's upside down Kingdom, the leaders are those who sacrifice and serve others, having chosen to humbly be on the bottom.

In *Leadership by the Book,* Blanchard, Hodges, and Hybels share some great insights into the heart of a servant leader. The way of leadership is simply a way to serve. As such, a servant leader will always have at his heart the best interests of those he leads. For a servant leader, people aren't the means to an end; people are the end.

Leaders who are servants first will assume leadership only if they see it as the best way they can serve. They're called to lead, rather than driven, because they naturally want to be helpful. They aren't possessive about their leadership position—they view it as an act of stewardship rather than ownership. If someone else on the scene is a better leader, they're willing to partner with that person or even step aside and find another role for themselves where they can better serve. They don't have the need to hold on to a leader's role or position if it doesn't make sense from the perspective of service. They love feedback, because they see it as helping them serve better. They truly have servant hearts, so their focus is to serve the cause, not to enhance their own positions. They freely follow their natural motivation—which is to serve—in whatever way is appropriate for the situation: as a leader, as a follower, or as a teammate.[4]

It is important to remember that position equals function, not value. As the senior pastor, I am no better than anyone else on the staff or anyone else in the congregation. We are all equal servants but with different levels and areas of responsibility. The moment you feel you deserve to be treated differently is the day you lose perspective of your servanthood. When you forget you're a servant of the people and begin to see them as your servants situated to fulfill your objectives, you are on the road to ministry disaster.

Servant leadership did not come naturally for me. For most of my life, I have been placed in leadership roles of various sorts. Inevitably, I used these positions for my own advantage and for my personal ego gratification. Instead of having the followers' interests at heart, I held the position for selfish gain. After coming to Christ, answering a call to Christian leadership and serving in pastoral ministry, I found that I now had a new heart to lovingly serve others. Yet often I still had the "me first" mind-set when it came to leadership.

Though I served people in many sacrificial ways, there was still that motivation of personal payoff behind what I did. It was easy for me to fall into the trap of seeing staff members and congregational members as a means to accomplishing my ministry ends.

The Lord has taken me through a process of coming to see and live out the "towel and basin" servant mind-set of Jesus. When it comes to ministry, I am primarily a servant. I lead because that is the best way I can honor God and serve people. My objective must always be pleasing the Lord and doing His will. It should never be for the purpose of achieving temporary and shallow earthly rewards.

In the words of Eugene Habecker, "The true leader serves. Serves people. Serves their best interests, and in so doing will not always be popular, may not always impress. But because true leaders are motivated by loving concern rather than personal glory, they are willing to pay the price."[5]

This servant mind-set impacts every other aspect of what a leader is and what a leader does. The reality of true leadership is that your rights actually decrease as you rise in the organization, while your responsibilities increase. A servant leader stewards this Divine call for the purposes of God and for the benefit of the followers. This section of the book (pages 27-40), along with the section on strategic planning for your church (pages 41-52) are probably the least interesting and most difficult portions of the book. At the same time, if you have never studied this kind of material, it could prove to be the most important. I've found that the absence of planning and goal setting are often the primary skills that keep hard-working pastors from being effective.

Key Four
You Must First Lead Yourself

> *Do you not know that those who run in a race all run, but one receives the prize? Run in such a way that you may obtain it. And everyone who competes for the prize is temperate in all things. Now they do it to obtain a perishable crown, but we for an imperishable crown. Therefore I run thus: not with uncertainty. Thus I fight: not as one who beats the air. But I discipline my body and bring it into subjection, lest, when I have preached to others, I myself should become disqualified.*
>
> 1 Corinthians 9:24-27

Leading others begins with leading myself. I can't take people where I'm unwilling to go. It rightly has been said that "we teach what we know but we reproduce who we are." If I am going to be the kind of leader the Lord desires me to become, I must first learn to lead myself. This includes finding God's purpose for my life, firmly establishing my core values, taking my life in that direction through goal achievement, managing my time, and paying the price for effective living.

CHARTING A COURSE FOR LIFE

Before he begins his masterpiece, a great sculptor will look at the stone he is to work on and already sees within it what he wants it to become. Our lives are a work of art, which take a lifetime to develop. It is important that we know what we desire them to become. In his book *The Seven Habits of Highly Effective People,* Stephen Covey talks about "beginning with the end in mind."[6] To me, the end in mind is the Judgment Seat of Christ (2 Cor. 5:10, 1 Cor. 3:10-16). I visualize kneeling before my Lord on that Day. I consider the words I want to hear Jesus say. With that Day in mind, I build my life so that when I stand before Him, I will receive the kind of commendation I desire and will have completed what He called me to do (Matt. 25:21, Acts 13:36).

Ever mindful of that judgment, I have drafted a set of documents on which to build my life. First, I have a list of fifteen core values. This list is based upon a Biblical worldview and includes all that I value most in life. Based on these values, I also wrote my life mission statement. This statement includes my life purpose and involves the seven primary life roles I fill. A copy of my life values and life mission statement can be found on pages 115 through 118 in the appendix. On a weekly basis, I review these writings (much like the captain of a ship would review his compass) to be certain I am on course to arrive at my destination. Each time I study the documents, I am forced to redirect my life (to realign my course) with the purpose I am pursuing. I like to keep journal entries of my progress and my setbacks along the way.

PERSONAL GOAL SETTING

One significant tool I use in charting my life course is goal setting. It is hard to overemphasize its importance. In 1973, Yale University started a twenty-year study in which they charted the future financial success of their graduating seniors. They found that the 3 percent who set goals when they left the university were worth more financially than the entire remaining 97 percent of graduates who didn't set goals.[7]

The apostle Paul spoke of the grand goal in front of him when he wrote, "I press toward the goal for the prize of the upward call of God in Christ Jesus" (Phil. 3:14). At the beginning of each year, I set both five-year and one-year goals. These goals must be congruent with my core values and my life mission statement. They are established after much prayerful consideration. They help me move from where I am to where I want to be. Writing down my future achievements is an act of faith. In a sense, I am prophesying my future.

I use the S.M.A.R.T. formula for goal setting. My goals are specific, measurable, attainable, written and time sensitive. I then make a step-by-step plan for their accomplishment. These plans usually involve daily and weekly activities. I pray through my goals on a daily basis. My goals and plans are written in pencil (actually on a word processor) and not in stone. I'm always adaptable and willing to make changes as they become necessary. To maintain a balanced life, I establish goals in seven significant areas of my life.

Devotional/Personal Ministry – My yearly spiritual goals include daily time in prayer, goals for reading and memorizing Scripture, days I'll spend in fasting, and a goal for the number of people I hope to lead to Christ through personal evangelism.

Every pastor should develop a spiritual formation plan. Each individual is unique and as such should develop a unique plan. Due to many personal weaknesses, I've found a vibrant prayer life to be essential to effectiveness in ministry. Though I've learned not to be a strict clock-watcher, I've found that I need an hour in prayer daily to survive and at least two hours in daily prayer to prevail.

A great benefit to the consistency of my personal prayer life is conducting a one-hour morning prayer meeting at the church. My experience is that I must make a daily appointment with God to consistently spend quality time with Him in prayer and in His Word. I treat that appointment with greater respect and diligence than any other appointment on my schedule. Because I am meeting with God, early morning hours are spent without the interruption of phone calls or other appointments.

It has also been beneficial for my spiritual life to plan a yearly prayer retreat and an extended time of fasting. The fast for me means a slowdown on my normal ministry schedule, a fast from food, and also a fast from all secular media. It is a special and sacred time for me where I am emotionally refreshed and spiritually recalibrated.

Physical – Our bodies are the temple of the Holy Spirit (1 Cor. 6:19), and we will be held accountable for how we steward them. As such, I set goals for eating, exercise, and rest. Self-control, wisdom, and exercise, not fad diets and pills—are the keys to weight control and good health. I try to eat a balanced diet, limiting my intake of high fat and high sugar foods, while eating generous portions of fruits and vegetables daily. Several glasses of water and a high anti-oxidant multiple vitamin are part of my daily intake. Three cardiovascular exercise sessions of at least twenty minutes, two thirty-minute sessions in the weight room, along with daily stretching and abdominal exercises make up my exercise schedule.[8]

I'm not training for a marathon or to be Mr. Universe, but I do want to be a good steward of my body. Occasionally, when I break my routine for a couple of weeks, I experience less restful sleep, greater fatigue, and a lack of overall well-being. Every minister of the gospel should be a good steward of his or her body. Moderation in eating and a regular walking schedule may be a good starting place. Pastors at First Assembly are held accountable to maintain a regular exercise routine.

Family – What does a man gain if he wins the whole world and loses his own family? My family goals involve nurturing those relationships. This includes a weekly date with my wife and regular times spent together in prayer.

Ministry – My ministry goals are the corporate goals for the church. I make them my own objectives.

Financial – Every pastor should have a financial plan, yearly financial goals, and a plan for long-term financial management. I include both giving and savings goals.

Educational – I include books read and audio-teaching tapes listened to, along with formal educational accomplishments in my goals. It has been said, "One hour of study per day on any subject will make you an authority in three years, a national expert in five and an international authority in seven."[9] One of my educational objectives is to be a continual learner for the rest of my life.

Recreational – I don't always accomplish it, but I have a goal of playing at least nine holes of golf every week. It is something that for me is relaxing, enjoyable, and gets my mind off my normal responsibilities. I believe every pastor needs a recreational activity that accomplishes these objectives. I've also learned the value of taking a weekly Sabbath. If I don't, I eventually pay for it. It's important; after all it is one of the Ten Commandments.

Five days a week, I attempt to pray over my list of goals. I ask the Lord to purify my goals, redirect me if I need to modify them, accomplish them through me, and allow me to grow into His image and glorify Him through the goal achievement journey. This also keeps the goals in the forefront of my mind.

TIME MANAGEMENT

Your time is your life. As such, a vital part of leading yourself is managing your time. All of us have been given twenty-four hours a day. It is critical that we prioritize our time so that we spend the majority of it on those items most valuable toward accomplishing our God-given purposes. According to the Pareto Principle of time management the top 20 percent of your priorities will give you 80 percent of your results. You must know your top priorities and utilize your resources on them.[10] Applying this principle enables me to make the very best use of my time.

Planning your day in advance is a great key to effective time management. One moment of planning saves three to four in implementation.[11] Each day I make a list of the activities to be accomplished. I then place them in one of four quadrants.[12] The first is the "Significance" quadrant. These are those items that will give my life significance. They include my devotional life, relationship building, strategic planning, and personal growth activities. I put these items in a separate priority category, which I not only place within my "to do" list, but also schedule into my calendar. That way I no longer simply "try" to make time for them. Instead, I have already blocked out time for them daily. Most of these activities I accomplish between 5:30 AM and 11 AM. It is time blocked out apart from phone calls and other appointments.

The second I call quadrant "A," and I list it as such in my day-planning tool. "A" items are those activities that are important and urgent. Quadrant "B" holds important activities which are not urgent. The "A" and "B" activities are items that I believe I'm required to do. I'm the one in the organization who should be doing them. They give me the greatest return for my effort. These are the items that most benefit the organization. These activities are those which are most rewarding to me (the tasks I most enjoy). When a certain activity is required, gives a great return, and is personally rewarding, it goes to the top of my priority list.[13] Quadrant "C" items are all the items of low importance.

Within each quadrant, I numerically list the activities in order of their value. Then, I accomplish and check off completed items according to their priority. I've learned that I can't accomplish everything on my list. If I stay in the "Significance," "A" and "B" categories, I will accomplish the activities that give the biggest return. I delegate or eliminate the items in the "C" category. I try to constantly ask, "What am I doing that someone else could be doing?" Because I have a quality staff and a competent administrative assistant, I'm able to hand off a large portion of the activities necessary for accomplishing my ministry.

The greatest time management question I have ever used is a simple prayer, "Lord, what is the best use of my time right now?" In conjunction with the list I construct each morning, I am able to daily accomplish the Lord's purpose by following my heart after asking that simple question.

Then if I can keep a focused sense of urgency, I can accomplish a good amount of priority work in a relatively short time. It also seems the faster I work, the more energy I have for the task. I'm not simply working harder, but I'm working smarter. Many time management programs offer numerous time-saving ideas. To conclude this section, I have listed a few which have been the most significant to me:

❑ Eliminate the notorious time wasters of television and the Internet. They can both be wonderful tools or horrible time wasters. It is estimated the average American watches twenty-five hours of television each week.[14] I try to plan my television time using a VCR and limiting my TV time to a minimum.

❑ Learn to say no to what you shouldn't be doing. Remember that you can't do it all. You know what you shouldn't be doing by familiarity with your personal mission statement, core values and goals.[15]

❑ Delegate whenever possible. "Every time you do a job that someone else can do, you sacrifice work that only you can do."[16]

❑ Double use your time. An example of this would be listening to a cassette teaching tape while exercising.

CHARACTER

Throughout history there have been leaders of great influence with little character. This should never be true of the Christian leader. Before God uses a man, He wants to make the man usable. E.M. Bounds said, "God's plan is to make much of the man, far more of him than of anything else. Men are God's method. The Church is looking for better methods; God is looking for better men."[17]

I've decided to make character the first priority of my leadership development program. Without Godly character, every other leadership gift, talent, or skill is inconsequential in the long run. Billy Graham said, "Integrity is the glue that holds our way of life together. We must constantly strive to keep our integrity intact. When wealth is lost, nothing is lost; when health is lost, something is lost; when character is lost, all is lost."[18]

The Scripture teaches that we become like those with whom we spend the most time (1 Cor. 15:33 and Prov. 27:17). As I spend time applying God's Word and enjoying God's presence, I grow to become more Christ-like (2 Cor. 3:18). Practicing spiritual disciplines such as worship, prayer, meditation, journaling, fasting and Biblical study propel me down a character path toward Christian maturity. "God has given us the disciplines of the spiritual life as a means of receiving His grace. The disciplines allow us to place ourselves before God so that He can transform us."[19]

In addition, the close fellowship with others who are also pursuing Godly character has assisted me in my journey. I've found it essential to have a small group of men to whom I am open and accountable concerning my life. Continual growth in Christ-likeness is the most indispensable element of Christian leadership.

THE BARGAIN PRICE OF SELF-CONTROL

One of the great keys to leading myself is the ability to delay gratification.[20] I have a natural tendency to want to do what is fun, easy, and enjoyable and to want to do it now. When I give in to that urge, I never like the consequences. There is a price to pay for everything in life. You either pay the price now, or you pay it later. The problem with paying later is that interest has accrued. For example, it is easy to eat junk food and live like a couch potato. But the price paid later in sickness and a poor quality of life is higher than I am willing to pay. So, I pay the current price of proper eating and exercise habits. I'm always far better off doing "what I know I should do, when I should do it, whether I like to or not, and whether I feel like it or not."[21] This doesn't come naturally for me. I've asked the Holy Spirit to remind me when I wander off course. Through the Spirit's power I can come under Christ's control, put first things first, pay the price for significance, and accomplish the will of God for my life.

Chapter 4

STRATEGIC PLANNING

Key Five
Receive a Vision from God

Where there is no vision, the people perish...
Proverbs 29:18 KJV

Then the LORD answered me and said:
Write the vision and make it plain on tablets,
that he may run who reads it.
Habakkuk 2:2

Any enterprise is built by wise planning...
Proverbs 24:3 TLB

In recent years the subject of vision has become a hot topic and with good reason. You must have a vision. Tommy Barnett says, "Vision enables one to look into the distance with God and see what He sees and discern what is in His heart."[1]

Barna reports,

"In every one of the growing, healthy churches I have studied, a discernible link has been forged between the spiritual and numerical growth of those congregations and the existence, articulation and widespread ownership of God's vision for ministry by the leaders and participants of the church. If, for whatever reason, you are attempting to lead

God's people without God's vision for your ministry, you are simply playing a dangerous game. It is a game that neither pleases God nor satisfies people. Regardless of the cost, get His vision for your ministry."[2]

I fully agree with George Barna. If you don't have a vision for where God wants to take your church, you must make it your first priority. Do whatever it takes to obtain a glimpse into what God sees your church becoming. You may need to fast, pray, and get away for a time of intensely seeking the mind and heart of God. If you cannot see God's vision for your ministry, you must question whether you are God's leader for the church. If it is true that everything rises and falls on leadership, it may also be said that leadership rises and falls on vision. Whoever has the vision for the organization and takes people in that direction is the true leader. If you're the senior pastor, you need to be that person. When the vision became alive not only in me, but in the hearts of our people, First Assembly began to thrive.

Before I assumed the pastorate of First Assembly, I began to ask the Lord to give me a vision for the church. While studying the book of Acts in the winter of 1992, God answered my prayer. I noticed that everywhere the church went, it had a profound effect upon that area. The believers "filled Jerusalem with [their] doctrine" (Acts 5:28). The church was said to be those who "turned the world upside down" (Acts 17:6). While Paul was in Ephesus, "All of Asia heard the Word of the Lord Jesus," and great revival shook the region (Acts 19:10-20).

The word that continued to run over in my heart was the word "impact." I sensed God was calling First Assembly to be a church that would impact Deep East Texas with the gospel of the Lord Jesus Christ. I believe the Holy Spirit revealed to me His dream for our church. It included the numerical goal of 2,000 by the year 2000. I truly believed we could have a service with over 2,000 in attendance by the year 2000 and could average 2,000 in attendance during the fall quarter of the year 2000. I knew that a church that large could transform the Deep East Texas region.

I had the vision burning in my heart, but I knew I would have to sell it to the congregation. I started by sharing my thoughts with my wife. Then, one by one, I presented it to a few key leaders. Next, I shared the vision with a group of intercessors. A critical event occurred when I shared it with twenty-five key influencers, who I had been training to be lay pastors.

Every time I communicated the vision, the more I believed in it and the more impassioned I felt about it. Those I shared it with grasped the concept with great enthusiasm. At the same time, the numerical goal of 2,000 by 2000 seemed to them beyond the realm of reasonable probability. The church was averaging less than 300 in Sunday morning worship, and there was not a church in the city averaging over 600. But I persevered in my faith and ignited theirs.

Finally, on a Sunday morning in the fall of 1992, I announced the vision to our entire congregation. I was thrilled by the eruption of excitement at the proclamation. There were those in our community who weren't so enthusiastic. I heard reports of people saying that "it could never be done" and "that pastor is crazy to think his church could ever do that." The people of First Assembly seemed undaunted. They were ready to do something great for God and were looking for a leader who was willing to take them to the mountain of God's purpose.

Over time, the vision became more specific. The deacon board and the staff helped me craft a statement. Our vision is: "To be an authentic community of believers in Jesus Christ who are impacting Deep East Texas and our world. We're a regional church and a Bible training center where people experience the living God, have their lives transformed by His grace, and are prepared for successful living. We're a church that is multi-generational, racially diverse, and impacts every aspect of our society." A full description of our vision can be found in the appendix on pages 124-125.

After First Assembly saw God's vision, we committed our time, energy, and resources toward its fulfillment. George Barna says, "Vision for ministry relates to the state of your heart and your willingness to commit every resource at your disposal to His service."[3]

I knew this commitment to vision had to start with my wife and me. Aubrey Malphurs says, "Of course, the leader's personal dedication to the cause is an absolute must in creating trustworthiness for the vision. Generally, the perception is the greater the self-sacrifice or personal risk of the leader, the greater the trustworthiness of the cause."[4] Kelly and I worked long, tireless hours, turned down salary raises, gave a large percentage of our income, and called out to God continually for the fulfillment of the vision. As we led the way, the people of First Assembly responded powerfully.

On October 31, 1999, the first half of the numerical goal was fulfilled. We saw 2,459 worshiping together in our Sunday morning services. First Assembly is now a regional church that has become racially diverse and multi-generational. We constantly see peoples' lives transformed, and we are truly having an impact on Deep East Texas. The church fell short of the goal of 2,000 in average attendance by the end of 2000. Yet, we saw God accomplish more than anyone seemed to think was possible. During that three-month period we averaged 1,787. Without the compelling vision we wouldn't have come close to this kind of growth. Only if you could have been there to compare the church of 1991 to the church in 2000 could you appreciate the miracle of this God-given vision.

Key Six
Invest Time and Effort into Strategic Planning

Leroy Eims says, "A leader is one who sees more than others see, who sees farther than others see, and who sees before others do."[5] It involves directing a group of people into a discovery of where they are, who they are, what motivates them, and what they should be doing. It is helping them see what they should become. It is determining how to get to the destination. Then it is leading the way on the journey.

Strategic planning for a congregation is hard and time-consuming work but it is invaluable work. A key at First Assembly was setting the church on the right course through strategic planning. Just as God has a plan for our individual lives that must be pursued, God has a plan for each local church that must be corporately pursued. The task of leadership is to direct the church in finding and following that Divine plan. Unless the pastor is pioneering a new church, it begins with conducting a ministry analysis.[6]

MINISTRY ANALYSIS

A ministry analysis of a church will enable the ministry leaders to determine how the church is doing, the strengths, the weaknesses, and the direction it is heading. When I came to First Assembly of God in Lufkin, Texas, I did some research, asked questions, and discovered we were a church that had no real sense of vision or purpose. The church had been on a ten-year growth plateau. Somewhere along the line, it had lost its sense of mission and destiny. It had adopted an inward focus and a maintenance mind-set. The people had experienced a good deal of strife, division, and heartache in its recent history. For the most part, the unchurched community was unaware this church existed.

At the same time, the church had some untapped resources. There was a strong committed core of people who were ready to do something significant for Christ. The church also had a nice physical plant. The sanctuary was small and the buildings were in need of repair, but the church had a minimal amount of debt and was located on thirteen acres of prime real estate. Shortly after arriving at the church, a survey was conducted to determine the general demographics and the preferences of the body. Knowing who already made up the church membership was a good indicator of the kind of people we could most naturally reach in the future. Having assessed where we were, it was time to determine what our shared values were.

CORE VALUES

Business writers Ken Blanchard and Michael O' Connor write, "Perhaps more than at any previous time, an organization today must know what it stands for and on what principles it will operate. No longer is value-based organizational behavior an interesting philosophical choice—it is requisite for survival."[7]

Church growth expert Lyle Schaller writes, "The most important single element of any corporate, congregational, or denominational culture is the value system."[8]

In his book *Strategic Planning,* Aubrey Malphurs offers these insights on the subject of core values. "Core values answer the question 'Why do we do what we do?'

Congregation's values speak to what is most important in the church's life. I define core values as the constant, passionate, biblical core beliefs that drive the ministry."[9]

At First Assembly we have put together a values statement. I served as the editor and received input from our denomination, our ministry staff, and deacon board in developing the credo. We agreed upon the four non-negotiable values recommended by our denomination and accepted them as our own. They are as follows:

❏ Every person has the right to a presentation of the gospel at his level of understanding.
❏ Every person needs a biblical moral compass to guide and protect him throughout life.
❏ Every believer has unique gifts to be developed and used to strengthen the Church.
❏ Every believer has a purpose in advancing the global mission of the Church of Jesus Christ.[10]

To these four we then added a fifth, which we feel is essential and placed it at the top of our values. The fifth value is:

❏ Every person is created to glorify God, who alone is worthy of worship.

There was a strong sense of unity that these are indeed the highest values of our church. They are the key values, which will drive our church. We also listed ten values we see as being unique to our church. The complete list can be found in the appendix on pages 121-122.

THE MISSION

After defining what motivates our course, we must determine what the church should be doing. It is critical that a church determines its God-given mission. In *Managing the Non-Profit Organization,* Peter Drucker states, "What matters is not the leader's charisma. What matters is the leader's mission. Therefore, the first job of the leader is to think through and define the mission of the institution."[11]

The mission of the church is clearly presented in the pages of Scripture. In his book, *The Purpose Driven Church,* Rick Warren says, "Leading your congregation through a discovery of the New Testament purposes for the church is an exciting adventure. Don't rush through the process. And don't spoil the joy of discovery by simply telling everyone what the purposes are in a sermon. Wise leaders understand that people will give mental and verbal assent to what they are told, but they will hold with conviction what they discover for themselves."[12]

At First Assembly I took our church leadership through a discovery of our Biblical purposes. Our lay pastors also led their small groups through a Bible study in which they discovered the mission of the church. Then on Sunday mornings, I taught a sermon series called *What Makes a Great Church.* In the series, I taught on our five Biblical purposes. An effective purpose statement must be Biblical, specific, transferable, and measurable.[13] The Lufkin First Assembly Statement of Purpose can be found in the appendix on page 123.

STRATEGY

Now that we know where we are, what motivates us to do what we do, what we are to do, and what we are to become, we must next determine a strategy to get there. Strategy is the process that enables your ministry to accomplish its mission and its vision.[14] There are many aspects to developing a strategy. You must determine who you are called to reach, what their felt needs are, and what kind of church can accomplish the task.

At First Assembly, we see ourselves as a regional church called to impact our community and to reach a diverse group of people. We made a strategic decision to focus our ministry style to reach the largest segment of our population area. Our priority is the unchurched. This is reflected in our music, our facilities, our advertising, and our Sunday morning services. In addition, we provide outreach and individual ministries for a diverse variety of people. Though our regional population is primarily lower middle class, we strategically focus on appealing to the upper middle class. This decision is based on the belief that people are drawn to the next higher level socio-economically, rather than to a lower level. We also believe we will attract some people within the upper socio-economic class of our community when they see the impact that their time and finances can create through a church that is alive and is making a difference.

We decided the value and purpose of our church that requires the greatest commitment is the evangelistic value. Therefore, our strategy involves an aggressive evangelism outreach program that we will develop through a process of time. Though we were unfamiliar with the term, we implemented what Jerry Falwell calls "saturation evangelism." Our goal is to "use every available means, to reach every available person, at every available time."[15]

As such, our evangelism strategy is diverse and aggressive. We will use every available means but focus on the method we sense God is presently anointing for our area. Strategies are employed to reach the heart of the African-

American population. A ministry was designed to bridge across cultural and language barriers to reach the Spanish-speaking population of our area. The church has used visitation campaigns, confrontational evangelism teams, servant evangelism, evangelistic dramas, evangelistic crusades, direct mail, television, radio, the Internet, Sidewalk Sunday School, busing ministry (still in infancy), and a community youth center. We attempt to ride the wave of what we sense God is doing and emphasize the evangelistic method we believe He is currently anointing.

The Great Commission is about more than making converts. It is about making disciples. As such we have also incorporated a strategic process for bringing people from membership, to maturity, into ministry, and out to mission. We have adapted the Rick Warren "Purpose Driven Church" baseball diamond model as our process of bringing people into discipleship. We assimilate new members, program, educate, start small groups, add staff, structure, preach sermons, budget, plan our calendar, and evaluate our ministry according to our five purposes.[16]

In addition, we have developed what we call our First Assembly Strategy. I wrote out the strategy using the acronym 1st ASSEMBLY. The First Assembly Strategy can be found in the appendix on page 126. These are the things we do to accomplish our mission and become what God has called us to be. Our members have been trained to use the strategy as an effective method of praying for the church. Regularly, the executive staff evaluates our programs and ministries to determine if we are carrying out our strategy.

COMMUNICATING THE PLAN

Vision must be communicated with clarity, consistency and creativity. The Nehemiah Principle says, "Vision and purpose must be restated every twenty-six days to keep the church moving in the right direction."[17] Once a year we have "Victory Sunday." It is a Sunday morning vision-casting service. Through drama, video, music, and preaching, we recast the vision and purpose of First Assembly. Every month, I attempt to reexamine our strategy with our church staff and evaluate the course of our progress.

We have adopted the symbols of the baseball diamond and concentric circles to illustrate our purposes.[18] They are displayed throughout our church, along with our purpose and vision statements. These symbols and statements are on manuals, posters, business cards, our Web site, mouse pads, mugs, and even on clothing.

We have developed, borrowed, adapted, and used slogans to communicate our plan. They include, "2,000 by 2000," "Profoundly impacting Deep East Texas," "Every member a minister," and "Bring them in, to grow them up, to train them for, sending them out." Our vision has been condensed to the slogan, "Experiencing God, transforming lives, building people, and impacting our world." Our complete strategic plan is thoroughly explained in our membership class. It must also be adhered to in order for a person to be received into church membership. A monthly evening service has been set apart and designed to minister to all of those in our church who are involved in ministry and to cast vision. We are continually thinking of new ways to communicate and explain the vision, so people can run with it.

Chapter 5

HEALTHY MINISTRY

Key Seven
Be a Healthy Person

> *For I will restore health to you and heal*
> *you of your wounds, says the* LORD...
> Jeremiah 30:17

In Genesis God set forth the law of reproduction, that everything produces after its own kind (Gen. 1:24). This is certainly true when it comes to the leadership of a church. As a young man planting a church, there was a good measure of spiritual and emotional dysfunction in my own life. That dysfunction soon became evident in the church I pastored. The immaturity, insecurity, and selfishness in me were reflected in the church body. The turning point came in admitting my great need for healing and renewal. I began to attack those areas of weakness and dysfunction in my character and personality.

First I did it through prayer. I asked the Holy Spirit to uncover areas where I needed growth and I asked the Lord to heal those areas of my life. Second I applied God's Word to my life. I renewed my mind to my new identity "in Christ." I would find Scriptures that countered my unhealthy thinking and spent a good deal of time meditating on those Scriptures and affirming their truth in my life. When I would begin to act and think contrary to the truth of the Bible, I would immediately counter it with God's Word.

For instance, I had engrained in my thinking that my personal value was based on my performance and people's approval. When I began to react to life in that way, I would stop myself by remembering what God said about me. I would declare, "I am accepted in the Beloved" (Eph. 1:6). I would remind myself that I was valuable because I was made in the image of God and purchased by the blood of Jesus Christ (Gen. 1:27, 1 Pet. 1:18-19).

Every unhealthy area the Lord showed me, I confronted with prayer and God's Word. Over time my thinking processes and my patterns of handling life began to line up with the truth of Scripture. I literally began to become a different person (Rom. 12:1-2). By the time I was called to pastor First Assembly, God had accomplished a restorative work in my life and my health and wholeness as a leader was evident in the ministry.

Key Eight
Be Real, Be Relevant, and Have Fun

I have to admit that a lot of pastors I've known are not the kind of people I'm naturally attracted to. Many tend to be stuffy, pious, and seem to think phoniness is next to godliness. From such men, I most definitely want to stay away. Jesus in the Gospels sounds like a blast to hang around. The Pharisees on the other hand seem like they would be miserable company. Frankly, I think the Church in America often acts more Pharisaical than Christ-like.

Early on in the ministry, I took myself too seriously and tried too hard to impress people with my spirituality. I learned that people weren't drawn to that. It didn't produce life. I did an exit interview with one young man that was leaving my first church. He told me his reason for leaving was because he couldn't connect with me. To him, I seemed "too perfect" and "too spiritual." I didn't see myself that way, but I obviously presented that image to the members of my congregation, and they couldn't relate to me and therefore had a hard time receiving from my ministry.

I've learned that my ministry is strongest when I pastor from my weaknesses. Instead of only sharing my victories and successes, I let people also know my struggles and defeats. They need to know I fight the same battles they do and I don't win them all either. It is also important to preach and teach on subjects that actually matter in people's lives. When our audience hears us speak, they ask, "Is he going to be interesting?" and "Is what he says going to apply to my life?" I'm not talking about preaching a constant stream of "how to" messages but rather taking the grand truths of God's Word and demonstrating how they are interesting and relevant to the twenty-first century.

Ministry is hard, sometimes grueling, and often heartbreaking work. If you aren't careful, you can find yourself becoming sour, gloomy, and miserable. Life is too short to live that way. I made a decision to make ministry fun. At First Assembly, we rarely ever have a board meeting, staff meeting or church service without including some fun and laughter. I've talked to pastors with various sicknesses and ailments. I believe most of these ailments are due to job-related stress and a lack of laughter. Instead of getting medicated, they need to start having fun. Proverbs 17:22 says, "A merry heart does good, like medicine." When you laugh and have fun together, there seems to be a greater sense of harmony, cooperation, and enjoyment in the work.

Key Nine
Work Hard

I've found that it requires focused effort to accomplish great things in God's Kingdom. We are colaborers with Christ. I like the old adage "Nothing works, unless you do." Proverbs 12:24 TLB says, "Work hard and become a leader; be lazy and never succeed." If a pastor is unwilling to put great work into his ministry, he shouldn't expect to see great results (Col. 3:22-23, Gal. 6:7). I've known pastors who play golf six to eight times a month, take four to six weeks of vacation a year, and spend most of their workday fellowshiping with other believers, or aimlessly surfing the Internet and then wonder why they aren't seeing greater results in their churches.

My most involved lay people invest six to ten hours a week at the church, in addition to their forty-plus-hour work schedule. As such, I expect my pastors to work at least forty-five to fifty hours per week at church or in ministry related activities. Of course, with any such guideline, there is also a balance. For the first seven years of my ministry at First Assembly, I typically worked sixty to seventy hours per week. I also took less than a week of actual vacation time each year.

This wasn't healthy for my family or me. Through a series of situations, my work schedule became a forty-five to fifty-hour-a-week routine, and I started taking more time for rest and relaxation away from the church. To my surprise the church seemed to become the healthiest and the most effective it had ever been. There are seasons in the ministry of a church where long hours are required, especially at the inception of a new work. Yet, as a general rule I have found that when I am routinely working over fifty hours a week, I've gotten my focus off the fact that it is God who builds the church and I've started thinking it is Todd who builds the church.

There are some other general guidelines I have for the work schedule of staff pastors. From the beginning of their ministry at the church, I let the pastors know that I trust them and expect great things out of them or I wouldn't have hired them. As such they are given a great deal of liberty with their schedules. They are reminded of the importance of their time with the Lord and with their families. Some of the best hours for pastoral ministry are in the evening; therefore, they are asked to divide their workday into two parts. So, if they work late into the evening on a Wednesday, they are at liberty to come into the office late in the morning or take off early in the afternoon on Thursday. I encourage them to work forty-six to fifty hours per week, but I do not keep them on the time clock or in any way make them account for how they spend their time.

The bottom line is effectiveness. As long as they are healthy people, with a healthy and growing ministry, producing vital and life-changing results, I pay little attention to the hours they keep each week. On the other hand, if I see personal problems, ministry underachievement, or obvious abuse of liberty, I am quick to bring leadership and control to their schedule. I have had to do this, but it has been rare. For the most part, our pastors have always been people strongly dedicated to the cause of Christ and ministers who have loved what they were doing. As such, there have also been times I've had to ask some of them to take some extra vacation time for the purpose of personal rejuvenation and as a burnout preventative.

Ministry is often hard work, but it should always be work out of rest. I think it is interesting that the Levitical priests weren't to clothe themselves with anything that made them sweat (Ezekiel 44:17-18). Though they were to work; they weren't to sweat. I see that as the work of ministry. It is work—and it can be hard work—but it is work out of rest, the rest that Christ gives. I love the cause of Jesus, and I love the people God has given me to minister to (2 Cor. 5:14). It is also my desire to operate out of Christ's strength and His ability (John 15:5). When I am doing these things, the work of ministry doesn't seem like work. There is peace, and joy and rest in the midst of the work.

I wish I could say this is always the case, but for the most part it is, and that is the way God has designed it to be. When it works that way, there is no need for the rigors of scheduling, accountability, and time cards. Instead, the biggest challenge becomes learning to pull away to give other important things in your life the priority they deserve.

Key Ten
Learn from Others

There are many people to whom I have to give credit for contributing to any success I've experienced in ministry. This is because I've learned from so many. Many of them I have never met, but I have read their books, listened to their teaching tapes, and attended their seminars. In my first pastorate, I thought being creative meant coming up with ideas and concepts no one else had ever implemented. At First Assembly I redefined creativity as finding proven ministry principles and practices, then creatively implementing them to fit my church and the area of the country where I minister.

I also believe we only stop growing when we stop learning. As such, I made a decision early in my ministry to become a "learning machine." Throughout my ministry, I've always spent the best hours of my day in prayer and study.

We live in a day when learning has never been so easy. Through books, audiocassettes, seminars, distance education seminaries, and the Internet, everyone has a wealth of information and knowledge within easy grasp. Anyone can become an expert in his or her field of ministry.

Key Eleven
Keep the Church in Balance

I grew up in the state of Kansas. Often as you travel across western Kansas, you will see tumbleweeds dancing across the prairie. A south wind will blow and they will all head south. Then the wind begins blowing from the east, and they all go promenading eastwardly. As I look at those tumbleweeds, I see many people in the body of Christ. I have seen many sincere Christians blown here and there by the latest spiritual fad or the newest breakthrough doctrine (Eph. 4:14). These believers never accomplish anything significant in the kingdom nor have stability of life and convictions. I do not mean this as an insult but as an encouragement for pastors to keep a balance and not be thrown off by every new thing.

I've mentioned the importance of getting involved with what God is doing, but that does not mean every novel innovation, successful program, or new emphasis should be embraced by your church. I believe the Lord will raise up leaders with a message and the message will sometimes turn into a movement. I've found that there is usually something I can learn from such groups, but I would lose God's purpose for my ministry if I tried to fully embrace what each is doing.

I've known pastors who are into something new almost every year, and they never seem to develop the kind of church God really has for them. Ecclesiastes 7:18 NIV says, "It is good to grasp the one and not let go of the other. The man who fears God will avoid all extremes." I think that is a good word for pastors.

One reason for our consistent growth at First Assembly is balance. We try to learn all we can from other churches and other movements without losing our Biblical balance. I believe this philosophy of balance produces both people and churches that are stable, confident, and healthy.

In his book *The Purpose Driven Church,* Rick Warren does an exceptional job of evaluating different kinds of churches and explaining a balanced, purpose-driven model. Over the past ten years, we have followed a similar philosophy at First Assembly. We believe a healthy church glorifies God through worship, evangelism, discipleship, ministry service, and Godly relationships. We continually try to improve all five of these Biblical purposes in our church.

The same is true with our pulpit ministry. There is an attempt to balance topical and expository teaching. I work hard to teach on a wide variety of Biblical topics, keeping my messages in Biblical balance and away from overemphasizing any individual doctrine or subject. As in other aspects of ministry, balance is critical. I believe pastors should maintain a balance of doctrine, purpose, and even style.

At First Assembly, we have a creative team that works to design and program our Sunday morning services. We also work together to determine subjects to be covered. It is important to us that we give our congregation a balanced diet of teaching. Preaching in an evangelistic church needs to have the balance of bringing conviction to the lost and edification to the believers, as well as providing "milk" to the new converts and "meat" to the mature saints. This is not an easy task but I make an intentional effort to prepare messages that accomplish all of these objectives.

A balance of preaching styles is also important to me. This includes a balance of topical and expositional messages. It also means bringing variety by using video clips, drama, and illustrated presentations to present God's Word. One way we accomplish these goals is by varying our styles and target audience based on the service. Sunday morning messages tend to be topical, shorter in length, filled with more humor and illustrations, stronger on their evangelistic content, with the primary target being seekers and new converts. Wednesday evening messages tend to be expositional, slightly longer in length, deeper theologically, and primarily aimed at the fully convinced and mature believers.

Two Sunday evenings each month are designated for people to attend small group meetings. On the other two Sunday evenings, we have worship services on the church campus. Each has a vastly different purpose than the other. The first we call our "Miracle Night." It reflects our Pentecostal tradition. On those evenings, we have extended worship, a faith-building sermon, and prayer times at our altars. These prayer times are normally for healing, deliverance, and for receiving the baptism of the Holy Spirit. Some people say this is their favorite service of the month. The other Sunday evening service each month is a ministry rally. We highlight ministries, give away awards, and cast vision. I also share a leadership teaching designed for current and aspiring ministry leaders.

Chapter 6

OUTREACH

Key Twelve
Be Outreached Focused

> *Go therefore and make disciples of all the nations,*
> *baptizing them in the name of the Father and of the*
> *Son and of the Holy Spirit, teaching them to observe*
> *all things that I have commanded you; and lo, I am*
> *with you always, even to the end of the age.*
> Matthew 28:19-20

I personally have a conviction that all churches should be outreach focused. The departing words of Christ just prior to His ascension were marching orders for His Church to be outreach focused (Mt. 28:18-20, Mark 16:15-20, Luke 24:46-49, John 20:21, and Acts 1:8). In Matthew 28:19, Jesus commanded us to go and make disciples, not to stay and focus on personal agendas or maintaining an organization. God absolutely loves and cares about lost people (Lk. 15). His mission in coming to earth was to seek and save that which was lost (Lk. 19:10). The Church of Jesus Christ should be just as impassioned as our Lord is about the mission of reaching those outside the Kingdom of God.

When a church decides to become outreach focused, it will soon discover new passion, unity, and momentum. The Lord wired His Church to function best when it is fulfilling His plan of world evangelization. Our attitude is tied to where we keep our focus. Spending most of our time thinking about ourselves always gets us in trouble. A church that focuses on itself soon becomes stagnate, selfish, and filled with complainers. If the church has an outreach focus it looks to Christ for direction, wisdom, and strength; and it reaches out to a world that needs Jesus. As members see their families', friends', and associates' lives eternally changed, a new energy and excitement begins to permeate the church.

It is very powerful to see your church altars filled with lost people being reconciled to God. Christians become too busy with their evangelistic mission to complain about petty things. The church has a goal on which to unite and a purpose that is bigger than it is. Once a church starts down the path of being outreach focused, the momentum will begin to grow and church becomes an adventure. There is nothing quite as rewarding as playing a part in seeing lost people surrender their lives to Christ and being a part of them experiencing radical life transformations. When I look across our congregation and see the faces of the people I personally led to Christ, it is the most satisfying feeling in the world.

THE PASTOR SETS THE EXAMPLE

John Maxwell has taught us that "everything rises and falls on leadership." This is particularly true when it comes to outreach. If the senior pastor doesn't deeply care about reaching lost people, neither will the church as a whole. If the pastor has a passion for the lost, it will be demonstrated in his prayer life, his schedule, and his sermons.

An occupational hazard of being a pastor is becoming isolated from people outside the family of God. We work with Christians, most of our immediate families are all serving Christ, and our professional network is made up of believers. If we aren't careful, before long we have no relationships with the lost. To combat this tendency, a pastor must decide to look at life through Great Commission lenses. We need to see all the people with whom we come into contact as the objects of God's love who apart from Christ will spend eternity apart from Him in a real place called hell. This will affect the way we look at all those in our world.

My wife and I constantly challenge each other to maintain this mentality and keep the evangelistic fire burning in our souls. Our daily times of prayer include requests for lost people and those who have drifted from the church. We have developed casual friendships with the waiters and waitresses at our favorite restaurants, the service people who regularly wait on us, and the people who frequent the fitness club we attend. I will often ask them if there is anything I can pray with them about over the next week. When they share a request with me, I will write it down and pray for their request and their salvation during the next week.

Everywhere we go in our community, we are continually inviting people to our church services and outreach events. Over time we have had many come to the church and receive Christ. Others have later approached us to ask for prayer or to ask our counsel about a situation in their lives. This keeps us aware of lost people and outreach focused. I personally have a golf group at the church that meets twice a month. Every member is encouraged to bring the unchurched to play with us. I've also attended receptions for new physicians who move to the community. My purpose is to develop a contact with them and possibly a relationship where I can share Christ. There are many ways to connect with lost people, but you have to be intentional and relentless in your efforts.

From these testimonies you may assume that I am naturally outgoing and evangelism must be my strongest spiritual gift. This actually isn't the case. I naturally tend to be somewhat introverted and I really enjoy my time alone, but I have decided to be outgoing for the cause of reaching the lost. Teaching and leadership are far and away my strongest spiritual gifts. Evangelism falls somewhere between third and fifth, depending on the list you use.

My heart is very much that of a pastor, but Paul told Timothy to "do the work of an evangelist" (2 Tim. 4:5). That is something I constantly strive to do. Church members who see me out in public or go with me into the community observe my lead in doing the work of evangelism. Sometimes I will tell my evangelism stories in my sermons or acknowledge when a person who received Christ at our altars was someone Kelly or I had invited to church. This lets our people know that we are living out what we are asking them to do. Doing so isn't easy for me, and I will go through seasons when my evangelistic efforts wane, but God has a way of reminding me when that happens to get me back in the game.

I tell our congregation that it is no easier for me than it is for them. It requires effort to leave the isolation of the church office and parsonage. Also, when people know I'm a pastor, it can build an immediate wall to their receptivity. I also tell them that my Godly lifestyle is less effective as a tool of evangelism than theirs. People expect me to live right; they think I'm "paid to be good." When they do the right thing, it is really impressive, because people know they are "good for nothing." These testimonies and examples help motivate the average guy in the pew to make attempts at reaching out to those in his life.

MAKE OUTREACH YOUR HIGHEST PRIORITY

A church should maintain a balance in all five purposes of the church (worship, evangelism, discipleship, ministry, and community). Yet, to do so, evangelism and outreach must be given special emphasis. The reason is obvious. Each of the other four purposes of the church can tend to be very self-focused. I enjoy hanging out with my Christian brothers and sisters for fellowship. It is great to listen to Bible teaching, discuss the Scripture, and be discipled in the ways of God. There is nothing quite as satisfying as spending time worshiping in the presence of God. It is actually quite enjoyable and practical to serve my fellow church member through my ministry, knowing they in turn will bless me with their ministry. I can do all of these things without reaching too far beyond myself.

Evangelism and outreach are in another category. They require stepping out of my comfort zone and making personal sacrifices to reach out to people who are different from me. Left to themselves, a congregation will naturally move away from an outreach focus. It is the pastor's responsibility to keep the church focused on the Great Commission and our evangelistic responsibility. Being outreached focused isn't easy. It is expensive, it is challenging, it requires sacrifice, and it creates facility problems.

The only thing more difficult than staying outreach focused is becoming inward focused. Inward focus leads to lost momentum, internal conflict, loss of purpose, and stagnation. Personally, I prefer the difficulties that come with being an outreach-focused church. Also, the rewards of seeing changed lives and lost people coming to Christ far outweigh the cost involved.

All of our ministry departments make evangelism a high priority. Our Student Ministry Department of college, youth, and children's ministries all have significant outreach events. Even our Halloween night alternative called FAMtastic is an outreach event where we see people make commitments to Christ. While our church was still relatively small, we were known for having the best Vacation Bible School program in our city. Yet, the program was extremely expensive, volunteer-labor intensive, and we saw little evangelistic fruit. One year, due to a construction project, we had to abandon VBS and had a four-evening Kid's Crusade. Instead of two or three commitments for Christ, we saw dozens of children give their lives to Christ and many return the following Sunday. Due to the evangelistic value of the crusade, we have turned from VBS to the more effective Kid's Crusade. The Hispanic ministry of our church is another vehicle for outreach. We estimate slightly more than 50 percent of our English-speaking congregation's growth has come through conversion, while over 80 percent of our Spanish speaking congregation's growth has been by conversations.

If you want to become an evangelistic church, members of your church need to know how to share their faith. At First Assembly we constantly provide opportunities to be instructed in basic evangelistic skills. It begins with our membership class, where every member learns how to share their faith using the "bridge illustration," "the Romans Road," and their personal testimony. Our Mission 401 class includes a section on personal evangelism. Class participants are required to get involved in personal evangelism and to keep a journal on their results. Every year I teach a Sunday morning sermon series or a couple of messages on personal evangelism. We also offer a Yearly Sunday school class on the subject and an annual soul-winning workshop.

THE PRICE OF BEING OUTREACH FOCUSED

There is a price to pay if a church is going to be outreach focused. First is the comfort price. The staff and members of the church will need to get out of their cozy

Christian comfort zones to touch lost peoples' lives. As the church grows from all the new converts coming in, "long-time" members may lose their favorite spots on their favorite pews. You will end up with cigarettes butts in the parking lot; people who dress inappropriately; people with multiple body piercings, tattoos, and multi-colored hair; newcomers more familiar with curse words than with the word *hallelujah*; and visitors who don't act as civilly as most Sunday-morning worshipers.

Second is the people price. When we decided to become outreach oriented, not everyone liked it. We lost a good percentage of our congregation. Of course, their seats were quickly filled with eager newcomers. I've had some good friends leave our church because they didn't like the "rock" music, the crowds, and the emphasis on people outside the church. That can be painful.

It is even more painful when those who decide to stay sow strife and criticize the leadership. These people need to be confronted, and they usually leave the church. Actually, it is in everyone's best interest that they find another church. Yet, when they are people you care about, seldom do you feel like rejoicing over their departure. In our new members' class, Kelly tells her students not to become members if they are not fully on board with our outreach-focused vision. If they stay it won't be good for them or for the church. We also offer to give them a list of churches where we feel they would be more comfortable.

Third is the money price. There is a high financial cost to being an outreach-focused church. It is less expensive to keep sheep in the corral than it is to reach out to lost sheep. A large percentage of our yearly income and staff energy goes into outreach services, events, and tools. On a regular basis the commitment to be outreach focused is the

71

determining factor in our financial decisions. Recently we were in the process of replacing our acoustic grand piano with an electric keyboard. In a board meeting the discussion became whether we should sell the $12,000 instrument or keep it for our church fellowship hall. I had to quickly remind the board members of the number of people we could reach for $12,000. When it came to deciding whether to invest in the lost or have a luxury piano for our fellowship hall, the decision was clear and easy. We decided to sell the piano.

OUTREACH SERVICES

Though it has been evangelistically effective for many churches, First Assembly does not follow the "seeker-sensitive model" in our Sunday morning worship. We do, however, prepare our services with the seeker in mind. We work very hard to create a service that our people would be excited to invite their lost neighbors, employer, or family to. When considering what that service will look like, I ask, "What kind of service would I like to bring an unchurched friend or family member to?"

To begin with I would want them to feel accepted and respected. Second, I would want them to experience the presence of God. Third, I'd like them to hear the uncompromising Gospel in a relevant, convicting, and convincing way. Fourth, I'd desire for them to have a good time and want to return.

I wouldn't want them to feel embarrassed, bored, or rejected. I wouldn't want them to be subjected to self-promotion, fund-raising, inauthentic use of spiritual gifts, or to have to sit through a service that is irrelevant to their lives. At First Assembly we continually encourage our members to invite their unchurched friends to church. In return we work very hard to provide a service they would be glad they brought their friends to. This sort of "come and see" evangelism has become the primary way people come to First Assembly (John 1:46).

We believe those who do not know Christ can be deeply touched by the Spirit of God as they are among Christians genuinely worshiping the Lord (1 Cor. 14:25). In our membership interviews, many newcomers have said the first time they visited First Assembly is the first time they ever "felt" God, and that is what kept them coming back. At the same time, we realize most unchurched people are not prepared to stand through forty-five minutes of praise and worship on Sunday morning. Neither do we believe it takes extended times of worship to have truly glorified God and to have experienced His presence.

Typically our worship (which is contemporary in style) lasts twenty to twenty-five minutes, depending on what else is happening in our services. Periodically (about once a month) we will invite individuals to come to the altars to receive prayer during the last half of worship. Prayer teams will be prepared to minister to them during that time. We have had wonderful testimonies of answered prayer, healing, and deliverance that have come from those times. The Scripture tells us that God inhabits the praises of His people (Ps. 22:3). As we praise, it seems God manifests Himself in a special way to minister to people's needs. I've never heard any visitor complain or speak negatively of the practice. Instead many have been touched and ministered to by viewing or participating in this.

We give an offering disclaimer, explaining that for our visitors the service is our gift to them. The purpose is to help them understand that the church is not "after their money." Most Sundays we utilize the arts as well as pulpit preaching to communicate the message. We use drama, the choir, individual vocalists, multi-media presentations, and video clips to communicate. We rotate what form the individual arts take, typically having only one presentation per week. The key for us is quality and the anointing of the Holy Spirit.

My messages on Sunday morning are normally topical, though I will teach an expository series every year. I have a goal of speaking thirty-five minutes, though my messages vary from thirty to forty-five minutes in length. Throughout the year I will use illustrated sermons that we sometimes use as special outreach events. The message is followed by a capsule presentation of the Gospel and a "no pressure" altar call. Every Sunday we will have a response. Those who are not ready to come forward may fill out a perforated response card, which they will find in their bulletin and they can turn in at a table in the foyer. We escort new converts answering the altar call into a side room, where trained altar workers answer any of their basic questions, make sure they fill out a decision card, give them new-convert information, and pray with them.

We have a new believer's class, but it has been difficult to get new converts to the class on Sunday mornings. As such, we give every new convert their choice of a cassette teaching tape or VHS tape where I teach some of the basic information a new convert needs to know. If they will fill out the accompanying study notes and turn them in to the Welcome Center in our foyer, they will be given a nice hardbound Christian book as an appreciation gift. Many of our new converts take advantage of this opportunity. Those filling out the bulletin commitment card will receive all of the same information through the mail, as well as a follow-up phone call by one of our altar workers.

Early on in my tenure at First Assembly, I was tempted to give up on the altar call. We seldom saw people respond and frankly, it was a bit embarrassing. But we decided to keep giving people the opportunity to publicly profess their faith in Christ. When there was no response, I asked the congregation to join with me in prayer. I would pray that we would develop a greater heart for the lost, that each of us would become a part of inviting lost people to our services, and that those needing Christ would be drawn by the Holy Spirit to a saving relationship with Him. Over time God began to answer our prayers. Now there is rarely a Sunday service that someone does not publicly receive Christ as Savior.

In his book *Marketing the Church,* George Barna observed that one out of four unchurched people say they would attend church if a friend would just invite them. This is a statistic I regularly quote to our congregation. We promise our people an evangelistically effective Sunday morning service; and in exchange we ask them to invite their unchurched friends, family, and associates to it. To assist them we provide simple business cards that invite the recipient to worship with us. The card includes service times, our Web-site address, our physical address, and a map showing them driving directions to the church. Those who regularly invite people find it extremely helpful to hand them something with the vital information. For big events and productions, we will oftentimes provide complimentary tickets or special promotional flyers.

OUTREACH EVENTS

First Assembly has also had good success with big events and evangelistic productions. Over the past ten years, First Assembly has held several "Big Days" where we have encouraged our members to invite their unchurched friends to church for a high-attendance day. God likes Big Days too. In Acts 2, He started His Church with a big day, where 3,000 souls were added to their fellowship (Acts 2:41).

We have adapted the widely successful Friend Day program produced by Elmer Towns. "Friend Day" events create excitement, get our church into the habit of inviting others, build momentum, and bring in new visitors from the community. Our first Big Day was in 1992, when we set a goal of breaking the all-time First Assembly attendance record of having 425 in attendance. On that day we saw 466 join us in worship. In 2000 we had a Big Day where 3,228 worshiped with us in our main weekend services. Each time we see a large number of people make decisions for Christ, many new people begin attending our services on a regular basis, and the whole church has a sense of victory and accomplishment.

A good deal of planning, preparation, and administration goes into each Friend Day event. The Friend Day manual by Elmer Towns is a critical resource when planning such an event.[1] Dr. Towns was one of my professors at Liberty Baptist Theological Seminary and has had a very significant influence on my life. He told me research conducted on the results of the Friend Day program has discovered the most successful Friend Day events are those that remain the most faithful to the prescribed program. We have also found that to be true in our numerous Big Day events.

Instead of doing a typical Easter or Christmas musical production, we turn these Big Days into evangelistic events. We will utilize drama, music, and multi-media presentations. We have written some of the productions and others we have adapted from purchased scripts. We normally distribute free promotional tickets to the community through our members. These events have brought in a multitude of people and over time have allowed us to see thousands commit their lives to Jesus Christ. We have also opened up our support groups, marriage seminars, and other practical seminars to the community. Through these ministries many have visited our church services and eventually become followers of Christ.

SATURATION EVANGELISM

In addition to this come-and-see approach, we aggressively reach out into our city. Since our community is small we have adopted the "saturation" approach to evangelism. Our goal is to reach every available person, by every available means, at every available time. We are on local cable television with a one-hour program every week. The airtime was inexpensive, and through digital technology it is relatively inexpensive to develop a quality television production. We are on the air twice daily with a thirty-minute radio program. Our yearly radio and television budget is minimal compared to the effect it has had on our community.

Tommy Barnett is one of my greatest ministry heroes and a man who has been an innovator in methods of reaching the lost. We have adopted and adapted programs from his ministries at Phoenix First Assembly and the L.A. Dream Center such as Adopt a Block, Sidewalk Sunday School (originated by Bill Wilson), and Soul Seekers. We hold evangelistic cookouts in various areas of our community that are always well attended and quite effective for sharing Christ with the unchurched.

Every year we have a service outreach day, where we reach out to our community through servant evangelism projects and soft-drink giveaways. One year we had a free garage sale for low-income families in our community. Our church members donated thousands of dollars worth of clothing and merchandise, and we gave it all away at no charge. Hundreds of people received useful items and a free sack lunch. Few ever visited our church, but many saw that God and His Church loved them.

The church has served free meals for Thanksgiving and Christmas, providing an enjoyable Gospel presentation. In addition, the church gives away both food and presents to low-income families during the Christmas season. We also have active prison and nursing-home ministries that are primarily evangelistic and a small bus ministry that we hope to expand in the future. These are just part of the outreaches we have done through the years. Some of the outreach events we created while other programs have been transplanted from other ministries and adapted to fit our city and our church.

Chapter 7

CHURCH GROWTH

Key Thirteen
Intentionally Assimilate Newcomers

*Then the word of God spread, and the number
of the disciples multiplied greatly...*
Acts 6:7

I've never met a pastor who wouldn't like to have his church grow numerically. I'm sure there are some tired, burned-out, apathetic ministers who wouldn't desire church growth, but I've never had anyone confess it to me. Normally, pastors do want their churches to grow, but they don't know how to make it happen. I do believe that as a general rule, healthy churches will tend to grow. At the same time, I've known churches that appear relatively healthy but seem to have trouble maintaining sustainable growth.

I've heard pastors of plateaued and declining churches make some interesting statements. One told me, "If even 25 percent of the people who visit our church would stay, no building in town could contain our crowds."

Another one said, "It seems like our church has revolving doors. A lot of people come in, but at the same time, just as many leave."

Outreach-focused churches typically have wide-open front doors, but they also need to have very small back doors. At First Assembly we work hard to minimize the back door. Yet, no matter how hard you try, you will lose some people. In a typical church, every year 1 to 2 percent of the congregation dies. This is a fairly legitimate reason to leave a church! Another 2 to 3 percent transfer their church membership, often due to moving out of town. Finally and sadly, it is estimated that 2 to 6 percent of the people leave the church without uniting to another church body. So typically a church will lose 5 to 11 percent of its regular attendees every year, which means they will have to grow 5 to 11 percent just to stay even.[1]

It doesn't require a high IQ to realize church growth requires having more people become part of the church than you have leave the church. If a church can accomplish that feat to even modest levels, significant church growth is easily attainable. If a church will have a net growth of just 7 percent per year, it will double in ten years. If a church will have a net growth of 10 percent per year, it will double in only seven years. Many churches have enough new visitors to easily achieve these numbers, but they must learn to close the back door by turning visitors into members. I'd like to share the process of assimilation we use at First Assembly. It is based on four principles. They are the principles of anonymity, caring, belonging, and tracking.

People list their three greatest fears as the fear of going to a party with strangers, the fear of giving a speech, and the fear of being asked personal questions. I didn't understand the principal of anonymity at my first church, and I seemed to do everything in my power to violate it. Instead of emphasizing evangelism through the normal web of relationships in our church, we spent a great deal of time, energy, and money inviting total strangers.

When people came into our church, they felt like total strangers, because they were total strangers. Fear one down, two more to go. As I noticed visitors in our congregation, I would ask them to stand up and tell us their names. That's two for two. There was even a time when I would begin to ask them questions from the pulpit, "to help them feel comfortable and welcomed." Little did I realize that I had just exposed our guests to their three greatest fears and had done everything in my power to ensure they would never return. It seemed to work quite well, because despite a huge visitor flow, our church was not growing.

The principle of anonymity says that visitors want anonymity, but they do not want to be ignored. They like being greeted and feeling welcomed; but for the most part, they do not like to stand up, speak up, sign up, or pay up.[2] As such, at First Assembly we do not require any of these things of our new attenders. They are warmly greeted at the door. Various pastors and members wander throughout the facility, meeting people and welcoming them. One time I asked a person with an unfamiliar face, "Is this your first time?" When I did, it was obvious they were deeply hurt by the question, as they responded, "Pastor, don't you recognize me? I've been coming here for four months."

That is when we changed the way we greet people. Instead of asking the risky question, "Is this your first time here?" we ask those we don't recognize, "How long have you been attending First Assembly?" Newcomers say, "This is my first time." Long-timers are proud to say, "I've been coming for over a month."

As they enter the worship auditorium, an usher will help them find a seat (visitors often come late). During the offering we acknowledge all of our first-timers (without making them stand). We welcome them as a corporate group and let them know how delighted we are to have them join us by enthusiastic applause. They are told that they are not expected to give in the offering because the service is our gift to them. In exchange we do ask them to fill out a guest card, which they will find in their morning bulletin, and place it in the offering plate. Most seem to like this idea because if they aren't giving, at least they have something to stick in the plate. That card is a very valuable commodity. Finally, our people have been trained to be friendly, and several people will say goodbye to each visitor and ask them to return as they leave the church facility.

THE LAW OF HOSPITALITY

In the time of the Bible, there was a strong law of hospitality in the Middle East. When someone showed up at your doorstep, it was assumed "God sent them." That person was an honored guest that God had entrusted to your care. At First Assembly we endeavor to live out the law of hospitality with all of our newcomers. Our visitors are our honored guests who the Lord has sent to us. They are given the best parking spaces. We have attempted to maintain two visitor-parking spaces for every hundred Sunday attendees, in our largest service.[3]

In Lufkin, Texas, we have more than our share of rainy days. On those days we provide umbrella escorts from people's cars. We are always certain the visiting parking spaces are carefully watched. When people walk up to the front door, our greeters are trained to say, "You are going to love the service today." Also in the foyer, our hospitality teams are ready to show first-timers to classrooms, the nursery, and restrooms. These teams attempt to give each newcomer a colorful First Assembly welcome brochure, which contains information about ways in which our church can serve them and their family. There is also a Welcome Center in the foyer where they can find additional information or assistance.

Studies have indicated that most people decide whether they are going to return to a church during the first twelve minutes of their visit. We work very hard to make those first minutes very welcoming. Our grounds are manicured and our facilities are bright, clean, and inviting. We've put special effort into making our ladies' restrooms and nursery facilities clean-smelling and looking immaculate. In addition to the physical atmosphere, we work hard to maintain the right spiritual and emotional atmosphere for newcomers.

On Saturday evening and Sunday mornings, our prayer teams pray for newcomers who will be at our services, and they specifically ask the Lord to reveal Himself to them and to meet them at the point of their need. Those on the platform are required to be emotionally up, rejoicing in God, even if they are feeling down. This isn't being hypocritical, but it is a "faith choice" to rejoice in the Lord (1 Thess. 5:17-18, Phil. 4:4). If they are unable to do that on a particular Sunday, we ask them not to lead from the platform. The pastor, worship leaders, and choir set the tone for the service and lift people up or bring them down. We come to the service prepared and move quickly between transitions, while attempting to be sensitive to any spontaneous guiding of the Holy Spirit.

As we have grown, it has also been important to us to keep the "family feel" and the personal nature of our Sunday morning services. My wife, Kelly, has a knack for that and keeps the "family feel" during the time when she welcomes the congregation and makes announcements. I strongly believe, "As goes the pastor, so goes the congregation." If I want my church to be friendly, I have to demonstrate friendliness. Before and after services, I roam the foyer, hallways, and sanctuary, greeting, meeting, ministering to, and praying for people.

FOLLOW-UP

At First Assembly we are relatively aggressive in our follow-up efforts, because it is well accepted in the East Texas culture. Studies have found that the retention of first-time visitors will drop 50 percent if you do not contact them within thirty-six hours of their visit.[4] Because of this, after their first visit we begin our assimilation process immediately. On Sunday afternoons a volunteer calls our first-time visitors and thanks them for their visit. It is a very brief, personal touch. Since we started this practice several years ago, we have never had a negative response to the call but many positive ones.

On Mondays cookie drop teams visit first-timers living in Lufkin and drop off bags of fresh baked cookies. They are instructed to thank the newcomers for their visit, invite them to return, and move on to the next home. They are instructed not to go inside, even if they are invited. Also on Monday, letters are sent out to our first- and second-time visitors. I include a hand-written note on the bottom of each computer generated letter, along with my personal signature.

Many churches contact their first-time visitors but fail to realize that the second-time visitor is even more strategic to reach out to. Studies have found that growing churches assimilate only 16 percent of their first-time visitors but the percentage jumps to 85 percent with second-time visitors. We give second-time visitors a gift card offering them a complimentary beverage from our church coffee shop.

Third-time visitors receive a hand-written card from me. Recently those cards have been computer-generated but have the appearance of a hand-written note, and I add my own personal touch. When a person visits the third time, they are serious about the church. I personally call many of the second-time visitors and most every person by the time they have visited the third time. A few times a month, my wife and I will invite new second- and third-timer couples out for lunch. These lunches have proven to be effective at helping newcomers determine whether First Assembly is the place for them. The majority of couples we have lunch with end up becoming members of the church. A couple of times, we have had the opportunity to lead them to Jesus Christ.

At First Assembly we try to strike a balance between letting them investigate at their own pace and letting them know they are wanted. All of this follow-up may seem like too much pressure for visitors, and it may well be where you minister. However, this method has been effective in East Texas.

TURNING VISITORS INTO MEMBERS

The term *assimilation* essentially means, "making insiders out of outsiders." That is our goal with every newcomer who walks through our church doors, and it is a job that never ends. Just because a person becomes a member does not mean our job of assimilation is over. Studies have shown that 50 percent of new members drop out of the church during their first year.[5]

From our best estimates at First Assembly, only about 10 percent of our new members leave the church the first year after becoming members. The biggest key to our lower ratio is our new-member process. When I came to First Assembly, becoming a member meant filling out a card and meeting the pastor. About six months into my tenure, we established a new members' class that developed into a thirteen-week course, covering an entire Sunday school quarter. Some may consider this too much instruction for a membership class, but it has worked well for us.

My wife, Kelly, leads the class and puts a great deal of effort into it. The class has a hard-working hospitality team that makes class members feel welcomed, cared for, and loved. Every student receives a notebook-style manual. Kelly uses Power Point and video clips to make the teaching come alive. The class has become our most popular and our best attended. We believe an attendee becomes a member when they decide they want to join the First Assembly family. The Membership Class helps them determine if their values are congruent with the church's values and if they are willing to make the commitments necessary to be a member.

First Assembly sets high expectations for our members. Every member must commit to attending regularly (we have an active membership), becoming part of a small group or class, taking up a ministry in the church, giving their tithes to the church, refusing to gossip or be divisive, and living an authentic Christian lifestyle. Through the class people develop friendships, which make them feel loved. They become part of a small group, which makes them feel accepted. They also get involved in a ministry, which gives them a sense of importance. By the time most members complete our membership course, they have developed a true sense of belonging. This is vitally important in assimilation because if people do not feel they belong, before too long, they will say "so long." The class concludes with a personal interview with Kelly and me, followed by a New-Member Banquet.

An important aspect of assimilation is tracking. I see tracking as an important ingredient of our pastoral ministry. In Luke 15 the shepherd knew if one of his sheep was missing, because he counted and tracked them. Proverbs 27:23 says, "Be diligent to know the state of your flocks, / And attend to your herds." Every Sunday we pass registration notebooks down the aisles and ask people to record their attendance. Our people have been very cooperative in this effort.

Without such a registration, it would be practically impossible to keep up with all of the flock. Through the registration sign-up, we are able to track second-time visitors, third-time visitors, and the ongoing attendance of all our regular attendees. We have volunteer ministry teams who follow-up on regular attendees who have been out of church for two or more weeks. Those missing two weeks receive a nice, hand-written note letting them know we love and miss them. After three weeks, they receive a call from a telephone minister who discreetly and lovingly learns why they have been out of church. Their answers and prayer requests are turned into the staff follow-up director. Those missing four to six weeks receive a personal call from a staff pastor.

Of course, there are some individuals whose attendance is so infrequent they only receive contacts if they have missed for several weeks. Interestingly, we receive numerous "thank you" responses about the follow-up ministry and have never received any negative feedback. In following this tracking system we have been able to know the state of our flock and take care of our people. On each of our active members, I receive a monthly report that tracks worship attendance, small-group attendance, Sunday-school attendance, giving (not amounts but times they have given), and ministry involvement. This has been a great tool to assist in determining the spiritual growth of individuals and of our church. It also helps our staff to determine those who are the best candidates for new ministry involvement and for new classes and groups.

Key Fourteen
Prepare for Growth

A certain woman of the wives of the sons of the prophets cried out to Elisha, saying, "Your servant my husband is dead, and you know that your servant feared the LORD And the creditor is coming to take my two sons to be his slaves."

So Elisha said to her, "What shall I do for you? Tell me, what do you have in the house?"

And she said, "Your maidservant has nothing in the house but a jar of oil."

Then he said, "Go, borrow vessels from everywhere, from all your neighbors—empty vessels; do not gather just a few. And when you have come in, you shall shut the door behind you and your sons; then pour it into all those vessels, and set aside the full ones."

So she went from him and shut the door behind her and her sons, who brought the vessels to her; and she poured it out. Now it came to pass, when the vessels were full, that she said to her son, "Bring me another vessel." And he said to her, "There is not another vessel." So the oil ceased.

Then she came and told the man of God. And he said, "Go, sell the oil and pay your debt; and you and your sons live on the rest."

2 Kings 4:1-7

In the story of Elisha and the jars of oil, we learn a principle that applies to church growth. You will only be able to receive what you make room for. As pastors, God will give us only as many people as we make room for. When our church was averaging 300 in Sunday morning attendance, we were quite comfortable. The sanctuary was full, but we only required extra seating on especially Big Days. We had just the right number of nursery workers, children's workers, Sunday-school teachers, and ushers.

The problem was that we were not prepared to receive any more people than we already had. At that point, we made a strategic decision to prepare to become a church of 400. First, we recruited and trained new workers. Next, we started a second, early morning worship service. We made room for 400 and soon we had 400. When we ran 400 we began to prepare for 1,000.

This required radical change. I knew it wouldn't come overnight, but I also knew that if we didn't plan for it, the church would never receive it. This began by teaching our church to have a big-church mentality. I had to rebuild the entire infrastructure of the church. A great deal of recruitment and training was required. It also meant making plans to build a much larger facility. When we started building our new facility, we had less than 500 attending each weekend. The day we moved into our new worship center, First Assembly was a church of over 1,000.

It wasn't an overnight explosion of growth. Rather, it was a natural result of making room for growth. The building didn't cause the growth. Had we simply built the facility, we would have been a group of 500 people sitting in a 1,000-seat sanctuary. The key is to prepare and make room for growth if you expect God to bring the growth. This may surprise some people, but twice in the past ten years, we strategically decided to hold back on our evangelistic intensity, recognizing that our structure needed to catch up with our growth. In those cases we had not made enough preparation, and we could not contain the harvest. If you want to grow, prepare for growth.

Chapter 8

PRAYER

Key Fifteen
Become a House of Prayer

...My house shall be called a
house of prayer for all nations...
Mark 11:17

If I were assuming the leadership of a new church where all the ministries were of equal quality and I could only invest myself into strengthening one ministry my first year, the ministry I would choose is the church's prayer ministry. U.S. Senate Chaplain Richard Halverson said, "You can organize until you are exhausted; you can plan, program, subsidize all your plans. But if you fail to pray, it is a waste of time. Prayer is not optional for us. It is mandatory. Not to pray is to disobey God." I consider the task of setting God's people to pray one of my most important responsibilities.

To mobilize a church for prayer, the senior pastor must lift up the value of prayer. This starts with the pastors and church leaders being people of prayer themselves. How can I possibly motivate and admonish my church to pray if I'm not praying? I make it a practice to spend at least an hour each day in prayer, with a daily goal of spending two hours in prayer. I'm conscientious to attend every church-wide prayer meeting I possibly can.

My pastoral staff is held accountable for keeping a daily devotional time that includes times of extended prayer. They are also assigned to establish prayer among their leaders and within their various ministry departments. Every week the pastoral staff joins together for at least half an hour of prayer. We pray for each other's needs, for our church body, for our nation, and for the nations. Each month the church deacon board gathers for a similar time of prayer. Every meeting we conduct begins in prayer, and oftentimes during the day, we will stop other activities to pray for an urgent prayer request or to pray for God's wisdom in a given situation.

This attitude of constant prayer has created an atmosphere of continual prayer at First Assembly. The first priority of our First A.S.S.E.M.B.L.Y. strategy is prayer. Every member is reminded of this on a regular basis. Maybe the best way to learn what a church values is to look at the budget of the church and see where it spends its money. Because prayer is so important, we include the prayer ministry in the budget of our church.

CHURCH PRAYER DIRECTOR

A key to developing a vital, church-wide prayer ministry is finding a prayer director. For me, this started by asking God to enable me to find such an individual. Then I started looking for someone with three key qualities. First, this person had to possess a loving and supportive heart for my wife and me. Second, the individual needed to have administrative gifts and the ability to mobilize people. The ministry of prayer director is an administratively intensive job. Third, the person needed to be a person of prayer himself or herself.

The person that immediately surfaced was a lady named Linda Yarbrough. After selecting Linda, I gave her a written job description that we created together. Then I gave her the job of assessing our current prayer level and the current prayer ministries in the church. She found that First Assembly had no cohesive prayer movement but was made up of a few unorganized prayer gatherings and one general church prayer meeting. Linda and I decided that we needed to have an integrated prayer ministry that worked with a central mission and vision. I made a commitment to support the ministry and to give her the resources she needed to start an organized prayer movement in our church. It was an elephant-sized project, but I let her take on the job "one bite at a time."

We started by implementing the pastor's prayer partner ministry that was designed by John Maxwell. From there the prayer movement began to grow one ministry at a time. Linda would start a new ministry, get it up and running effectively, then delegate it to a leader she had been mentoring for that purpose. Then she would move on to start a new ministry. Before long Linda had developed a team of leaders, all leading one of several prayer ministries in the church, which she directed. Linda started on staff in a volunteer capacity but worked her way into a paid staff position.

TEACHING ON PRAYER

Another important aspect of mobilizing prayer throughout the church is for there to be ongoing teaching on the subject. Every year I plan to do a teaching series on the subject of prayer. I typically do this series in January or do it in conjunction with a series on how to incorporate the spiritual disciplines in our lives. Then I ask for a prayer commitment from our congregation for the coming year. Providing time for regular testimonies to be shared from the pulpit or as part of a video announcement from people who have had powerful answers to prayer has encouraged our congregation about the effectiveness of prayer.

At least two Sunday-school quarters every year, we offer classes on the subject of prayer, and we have ongoing small groups whose emphasis is prayer. This provides a format to acquaint people with prayer disciplines such as silence, journaling, praying through the Scripture, and fasting. Our membership class includes a section teaching each new member the value and the practice of prayer. The follow-up class on maturity gives three full weeks of its curriculum to the subject of prayer and requires graduates to develop a personal prayer life.

PRAYER IN OUR SERVICES

We have endeavored to include prayer in our worship services. Forty-five minutes before our early Sunday morning worship celebration, prayer partners gather to pray with me. We pray together for the upcoming services, and they pray for my wife and me. We spread prayer times throughout our services. On Sunday mornings we have the congregation unite in corporate prayer for our time together and for each person in attendance and for pressing needs. This normally takes only one or two minutes, but it has a great effect on the service.

Throughout the services, intercessors, watching the service on video monitors in another room, fervently pray for God's will to be accomplished in our gathering. Following each message I will lead the congregation in a prayer in which we ask the Lord to help us apply what we have examined from His Word to our lives. At the end of service, following our salvation altar call, we have a prayer altar call for those wishing to stay after dismissal. Our staff pastors, lay pastors and trained prayer ministers are prepared to join with anyone desiring prayer or encouragement.

Every four to six weeks we will open our altars in the midst of worship to have people come for prayer with our pastors and trained prayer ministers. There have been powerful testimonies of answered prayer that have come out of these times. During other services we will join in extended concerts of prayer where a leader leads in united prayer for specific requests. Oftentimes we will break into prayer circles of four to six people praying together in these small groups.

PRAYER MINISTRIES

There are numerous prayer ministry opportunities available to the people of First Assembly. We have a prayer room that has been set aside for the purpose of prayer. In it there are maps of our city, our nation, and the world. Inspiring prayer posters are on the walls, an updated prayer list is available for those coming to pray, along with a list of missionaries and their nations.

Like many churches we have a prayer chain that is constantly operating. Our twenty-five-member chain has five calling captains who are assigned to each call five people. To keep the ministry active, we are certain to send at least one request every week, though we typically send more. I believe it is important to listen to the Lord's direction, be creative, and change strategies if old methods become stale. Over time we have conducted a monthly twenty-four-hour prayer vigil, all-night prayer vigils, forty days of prayer and fasting, early morning prayer services, prayer retreats, and a prayer request hotline for the community. At various times all of these prayer opportunities have been effective. The key has been finding what works for us at the time and being willing to try something else when the old method becomes ineffective.

KEEPING THE PRAYER FLAME ABLAZE

Throughout the year, there are a variety of ways in which we attempt to keep the prayer flame alive. We have an annual week of prayer and fasting in January, which we call "Sacred Assembly." It gets the church to start each new year seeking the face of God through humility, brokenness, and repentance. We corporately ask the Lord for His direction, wisdom, and blessing on the coming year. We pass out laminated bookmarks listing the First A.S.S.E.M.B.L.Y. strategy as a prayer track. On the backside it includes church-wide goals for the coming year.

Whenever we call for times of corporate fasting, we allow the congregation to participate at various levels. Some may drink only water, others only fast desserts during the period, and there is every variation in between. We will have a few people fast throughout the entire period and many who fast a few days or just one meal each day.

Over time we have found that it is important to have people sign up, listing their commitment. Some may object to this practice, but remember this is not private fasting but corporate fasting. I've occasionally announced my personal commitment to motivate others and to strengthen my own resolve. Each time of fasting has resulted in exciting breakthroughs in the lives of the people of First Assembly. We also hold an annual prayer retreat at a nearby Episcopal church for those who are active in the prayer ministry.

Through a vigorous and organized effort, First Assembly has been able to establish an atmosphere of prayer. Without that atmosphere the anointing and empowerment we have sensed on the other ministries of the church would quickly fade. I heard the story of five young college students who were spending a Sunday in London, so they went to hear the famed C.H. Spurgeon preach. While waiting for the doors to open, the students were greeted by a man who asked, "Gentlemen, let me show you around. Would you like to see the heating plant of this church?" They were not particularly interested, for it was a hot day in July. But they didn't want to offend the stranger, so they consented. The young men were taken down a stairway, a door was quietly opened, and their guide whispered, "This is our heating plant." Surprised, the students saw 700 people bowed in prayer, seeking a blessing on the service that was soon to begin in the auditorium above. Softly closing the door, the gentleman then introduced himself. It was none other than Charles Spurgeon. Without question, prayer was a great key to his powerful preaching ministry. If a church is going to be empowered to fulfill God's plan, it must have a vital prayer ministry.

Chapter 9

MINISTRY

Key Sixteen
Equip and Release the Laity

And He Himself gave some to be apostles, some
prophets, some evangelists, and some pastors and
teachers, for the equipping of the saints for the work
of ministry, for the edifying of the body of Christ.
Ephesians 4:11-12

Shortly after coming to Lufkin, the words of Moses to Pharaoh "Let My people go," (Exodus 5:1) were words I sensed the Lord speaking to me. First Assembly had many talented, gifted, hardworking people who had never been released for significant ministry. I told the Lord I would do all I could to assist the people of this church to carry out the ministries He had called them to.

Soon we had people coming to us, telling us the dreams in their hearts. As I listened to their stories, I shared with them how we would assist them to receive the training and find the resources to fulfill the ministries which their passions fueled. Soon, numerous new ministries came into existence. My wife and I began to talk with other people to discover what gifts they had been given, what experiences they had lived, and what passions the Lord had given them. Then we attempted to match these people with the ministries in the church where they could best serve. Over time we standardized this process, using diagnostic tools and interviews to place them into ministry positions. It became a requirement for becoming a member of First Assembly.

Since that time, I've discovered much quality material on the subject of mobilizing lay people for ministry. A few years back we did a survey and discovered that 70 percent of our membership was involved in ministry. I believe the reason we have had such a high percentage of involvement can be summed up in five steps.

First, we teach every new member the value of serving. Second, we have a stated expectation that every member will be a minister. Third, we help them find the ministry position that they will most enjoy and where they can best serve. Fourth, we give them training on how to effectively do their ministries. Fifth, we follow up on their progress with encouragement and additional training opportunities. Our success in maintaining these high levels of involvement has been directly related to how well we carry out these five steps.

Key Seventeen
Small Groups Make a Big Difference

As First Assembly has grown larger, we have worked hard to also grow smaller through our Sunday school and small-group ministries. Shortly after coming to First Assembly, I identified twelve men who I saw as teachable, having a heart for God, and having the potential to be leaders. Every Sunday evening before our evening church service we would meet together for prayer, fellowship, teaching, and discussion. I selected several books, which we read during the week and then discussed the next Sunday.

Through this group, I saw tremendous growth in some of the men. It seemed to bond all of them to me and to one another. After several months I introduced them to the idea of starting small groups with them as the leaders.

Over time, as I cast vision for it and discussed it, the men became excited about the idea. Finally, I asked them to bring their wives to a meeting with them where I shared with them my heart for the church and my vision for a small-group ministry. Eleven of the twelve couples got on board with the idea and signed on as group leaders. Another mature and Godly couple in our church was asked to fill the slot of the couple who withdrew.

I then announced the idea of small groups to the congregation. The group had decided it would be best to have small-group meetings twice per month and to meet the off weeks for training and discussion of how the groups were going. Instead of having them on another night, we decided to cancel our Sunday evening worship services on the first and third Sundays for small groups.

Each couple had to line up a host home, find an apprentice leader, and recruit members for their group. For the groups that wanted to participate, we provided childcare and children's ministry at the church for kids newborn through sixth grade. The groups with members having children at the church rotated their meetings at the church to assist the children's ministers. Parents were given times they could drop off their children and a time at which they had to pick them up.

Over the final two months, my wife and I conducted model groups with the leaders to model for them what their group should look like. The groups were to include a time of worship, testimony, prayer, Bible study, and fellowship. We continued to cast vision to the entire church body and provided informational material about the groups and their leaders.

In January of 1993, our groups started off with great success. Within three months, two of the group leaders decided they weren't cut out to be group leaders, but their apprentices or an apprentice from another group took their places. There were some bumps and struggles along the way, but by mid-1994 we had eighteen small groups. I finally turned over the leadership of the groups to an associate who had a difficult time maintaining what I had started. Soon we were back down to twelve groups, and some of them were on life support. Staff changes were made and a former group leader named Andy Salagaj became my associate pastor. For a season we worked together to revive the groups. Finally, the primary responsibility for groups was turned over to him. We also added youth small groups, support groups, and discipleship groups. Within a few years, we had over forty groups. Then we hit a two-year plateau and eventually began to actually see attrition in our groups.

In 2000, I visited New Life Church in Colorado Springs, which had developed a system called Free Market Cells. I brought the idea back to First Assembly. One of our staff members, Karen Norton, was given the full-time responsibility of working with Andy to administrate Christian Education and Small Groups. We adapted the idea of Free Market Cells by taking many of the restrictions and limitations off of our groups. The number of people in each group was then left up to the leader and the people in the group. Emphasis was then shifted to meeting the felt needs of people; therefore, a multitude of topics and interests became available in the groups.

People choose the type of group they want to go to based on relationships or an interest or a need they might have. We set clear starting and stopping points so that people sign up for a group knowing the commitment beforehand. The goal of our new groups is building healthy relationships between people, discipling believers to become disciplers, and providing the unchurched an unthreatening way to become associated with Christians.

During our experience with small groups at First Assembly, I've learned several lessons. First, it is critical that the senior pastor be involved in groups himself, continually casting vision for the value of groups and staying informed on the growth and health of the small-group system. Second, small groups require a great deal of attention. In a larger church at least one staff member should have the groups as his or her main priority. Third, people enjoy having a variety and diversity of groups. Fourth, group leaders must be given boundaries, accountability, ongoing training, attention, encouragement, and support. Fifth, the group leader should find a home other than his own to host a group. Sixth, if you want your group system to continue to grow, you must develop middle management for the group system. Seventh, you need to constantly make improvements if you want your small group ministry to continue to grow and succeed.

Key Eighteen
Invest in Leaders

I enjoy discipling, caring for, and developing friendships with the people in my congregation. Every week I prioritize time for prayer, study, leadership activities, and sermon preparation. From there I want to spend time loving, ministering to, and developing people. Yet, I can't do that with everyone in my church. As such, I try to pastor strategically. This starts with my pastoral staff. Every week we meet for a time of prayer, teaching, discipleship, and fellowship. I meet privately with four of these pastors at least every week. The pastoral staff also does special things together like going on prayer retreats, ministry conferences, golf outings, and sporting events.

The next level is my deacon board. These individuals make a significant contribution to First Assembly. In addition to our two to three meetings a month, they oversee significant committees in the church. We also meet monthly for prayer, teaching, discipleship, and fellowship. Every year I privately spend time with them, or Kelly and I will spend time with them and their spouses.

I am a caring shepherd to about twenty-five families in my congregation. This includes my pastoral staff, deacon board, some additional key staff, department leaders, and a few others. I know them and their children by name. If they have a need, I will personally be there for them. Should they be in the hospital, I will visit them daily. If their children get married, I am delighted to counsel the couple, perform the wedding, and attend the reception. With my other responsibilities, twenty-five families are just about all I can handle.

But as I have done that for them, I expect them to do the same for others. God does not hold me responsible to care for every member of my church, but I am responsible to make sure every member of my church is cared for. There are two pastors on staff who have pastoral care as one of their primary responsibilities. We also have care-giving ministers in the church who visit hospitals and support people in their times of need. We work hard to care for our church body, but my priority is caring for the key leaders of the church who in turn care for others. This is not a hard-and-fast rule, but it is a principle I typically follow.

We are constantly attempting to develop leaders. For anyone who wants to serve as a leader in the church, there is a track they can get on to develop leadership skills. Similar to the model in *The Purpose-Driven Church,* we have a 101, 201,

301, and 401 course. Our membership course called 101, focuses on teaching newcomers all of the commitments we expect from members of First Assembly. We have an intensive discipleship course called 201, that teaches what is required to grow as a Christian, explains the spiritual disciplines, and includes a mentor to help members through the process. Training and preparation for significant ministry involvement is called 301. It includes extensive diagnostic testing and a ministry apprenticeship. Finally, 401 includes training on personal evangelism, mentoring, leadership, and world missions. Students in 401 are required to share their faith and begin the process of mentoring a disciple in order to graduate.

Members of our church staff have worked with me to prepare the curriculum for each of these twelve-week long courses. Those who complete all four courses have not only learned a great deal about living the Christian life, but they have been required to put into practice what they have learned. Each person completing all the courses is acknowledged and congratulated by the congregation.

We conduct initial training courses for new lay ministers. Some of the training is quite extensive. Typically we provided a three-hour introductory training course, which is normally held on Saturday mornings or a series of training classes held on Wednesday evenings. Each month we have a Sunday evening service that is dedicated to celebrating the lay ministry of our church and teaching on the subject of leadership. Once a year we have a leadership retreat at a beautiful resort near Houston (two hours away). It includes fun, games, golf, boating, and shopping for those interested. In addition, it is a time of worship, ministry to our leaders, training, and motivation. Each participant pays for his room and some additional expenses. The church pays for the meals, decorations, door prizes, and a guest speaker. We put a good deal of money and effort into the event, and it is a time our leaders really look forward to.

Chapter 10

HIDDEN KEYS

Key Nineteen
Hire Staff from Within

I call this chapter "Hidden Keys" because it includes keys to our effectiveness as a church that are intangible and often unnoticed. Yet I believe they have been critical ingredients to what God has done at First Assembly.

The staff that surrounds a senior pastor can make or break his effectiveness. One of the greatest keys to the success of First Assembly is the wonderful staff God has surrounded Kelly and me with. The majority of our staff wasn't hired from the outside but was raised up within our congregation. One day I wanted to rate my success in hiring staff. After analyzing all of my hires over the years, I gave my hires outside the church the aggregate grade of a C-. Then I rated the hires we had made from within our congregation, and I scored us a straight A. Why would this be?

I think there are a number of factors. When you hire from within, you know what you are getting. I've found that when you hire outside staff, you aren't sure what you have until at least six months down the road. Résumés can be deceiving, references aren't always honest, and success in one place of ministry doesn't always guarantee success in another. When you hire active lay people, you already have seen their capabilities, their attitude, their work ethic, their character, and their gifts in action (Phil. 2:22, 1 Tim. 3:10, and 1 Thess. 5:12). For the most part, you know what you are getting, both good and bad. They have already bought into the church purpose, vision, and values. It also demonstrates to the congregation that you believe in them and that faithful and fruitful lay people can be promoted to full-time ministry positions. Another benefit is that it saves valuable time and money. There is no drawn out candidating process or the expense of relocating staff from across the country.

There are times when it is wise to look outside the congregation, especially for specialized ministry positions, when there aren't qualified candidates in your congregation or when you know of a high quality candidate who is worth the risk of bringing in from the outside. To develop such a "hire from within" culture, the church needs to constantly be mentoring and training members of the congregation. I challenge all of our staff to pour their lives into another person who could take their place if they left our staff. These efforts have not only benefited our staff but have prepared members of the congregation who have taken ministry positions in other churches and Christian organizations.

Key Twenty
Invest in Children and Teenagers

Studies indicate people under the age of eighteen are a group far more receptive to the Gospel than are those over the age of eighteen. Yet churches tend to expend the majority of their resources in adult ministry. At First Assembly we have decided to make a major investment in the lives of children and teenagers. At one time the driving force of our church growth seemed to be the growth and excitement happening in our youth ministry. At that time, when I was considering hiring an associate to assist me with adults, instead I decided to hire an associate for our youth pastor. It was a wise strategic move, as the youth ministry continued to grow and bring a greater level of momentum to our entire church.

We also invested in a 22,000-square-foot student center, complete with a video arcade and outdoor skate park. It was an expensive investment, but it has reaped great rewards in reaching children and teenagers.

Over time we have also learned that investing in children and teenagers often results in an opportunity to reach their parents. Many times the best way into a family is through the children. Some adults have started coming to the church and continued being a part because of the difference First Assembly has made in the lives of their children and teenagers.

Key Twenty-One
Get Involved in What God Is Doing

In his book *Experiencing God,* Henry Blackaby tells us to join God in what He is doing. That has been a key to God's work at First Assembly. When we have discerned God's movement, we have gotten involved in what He was doing. Many pastors hurt themselves and their church with their own sectarianism. "If it didn't happen first in my church or if it didn't originate in my denomination, it isn't anything I would be interested in."

In the 1990s, First Assembly became involved with two movements that brought blessing and growth to our church. The first was the Promise Keepers movement. Through the vehicle of PK, many men committed their lives to Christ and many others were motivated to become the men God wanted them to be. Our church embraced the Promise Keeper movement and used it as an opportunity to reach men and strengthen our men's ministry. Some would say we were just following the trend in the Christian community. I think we were simply getting involved with what God was doing.

In 1995, revival broke out at Brownsville Assembly of God church in Pensacola, Florida. The revival received great scrutiny and much criticism, but I find it difficult to argue with results. At last report the church had documented three hundred thousand people who had committed their lives to Christ through their evangelistic revival meetings. In addition, countless numbers have had their lives positively and often radically changed by God.

When I heard about what the Lord was doing in this church, I wanted to know whether it was truly genuine. If it was genuine, I wanted to be a part of it. My wife, a couple of staff pastors, and I visited Brownsville and experienced first-hand the reality of the work of God in reviving His Church. We returned to Lufkin, hungry for God and deeply desiring to see similar results in our church. God saw the cry of our hearts and answered us. For over a year, our church experienced a sovereign visitation of the Lord that helped shape who we have become and transformed many in our community. We embraced what God was doing and received a blessing for having accepted and participated in His move.

It is important to also realize that what God is doing in one location must be contextualized for another location. For instance, God visited our church in Lufkin in much the same way that the people of Brownsville Assembly experienced the Lord. Yet, we realized that what God wanted to do at Brownsville Assembly was different than what He purposed for First Assembly. As such, we never tried to emulate Brownsville. They were called to be a worldwide revival center. We were called to be a local church that was "in revival." There is a big difference in focus and method. At First Assembly we continued on the course the Lord had given us but with new life and empowerment. It is critical that what we learn and receive from others is always contextualized.

Key Twenty-two
Have a World Vision

First Assembly has made a commitment to do more than give to missions. We are a mission! At the same time, Jesus gave us a command to take the Gospel to every nation and to every people group. It is imperative that every local church has a world vision. It seems obvious that every local church should be investing an amount equal to at least 10 percent of its general fund for ministry to the poor, to bless other worthy ministries, and particularly to give to the effort of world missions.

Many churches do far more than that, but giving money is not enough. At First Assembly we endeavor to regularly educate our congregation on the Biblical imperatives of world evangelization and the progress the Church worldwide is making in this massive undertaking. At First Assembly we have an annual missions convention where we educate and encourage our congregation about its involvement in world missions. Annually I set aside at least one Sunday morning message to the subject of world missions. In our 101 class, we cast the vision for world missions and in our 401 class, there is an entire section devoted to the subject.

Through each of these avenues, we challenge our congregation to make prayer and financial faith promises to world missions. We periodically have a missionary share for ten or fifteen minutes in our services about what is going on in his or her field. For those missionaries particularly gifted as communicators, we invite them to bring a message from our pulpit on Sunday and Wednesday evenings. We attempt to educate and encourage our children and each age group through senior adults on their role in the Great Commission worldwide. Then we present to them different ways in which they can get involved.

Maybe the most life-changing way we help develop the hearts of our members for missions is through short-term missions trips. Annually groups from First Assembly are sent out to build churches, schools, orphanages, and minister the Gospel in foreign lands. During the past several years, we have sent out one couple and a single young lady from our congregation as career missionaries. Our involvement in missions and church planting are areas I hope to see our congregation elevate on our agenda over the next decade. As a church you can't do it all. Yet, if a church wants to honor God and be part of His redemptive plan for the world, a congregation cannot ignore its responsibility to be involved in world evangelization.

Key Twenty-Three
Keep Getting Better

A critical key to our ongoing excellence of ministry is the determination to keep getting better. In his book *The Winner Within,* NBA basketball coach Pat Riley said, "Excellence is the gradual result of always wanting to do better." Riley goes on to talk about his 1986-87 Los Angeles Lakers. That year each member of the team from the core members to the last person at the end of the bench was challenged to do better than he did the year previous. Each player was called on to put forth enough effort to gain one percentage point in each of five designated areas. Riley told them, "Don't try to go 10 percent above it. And don't let yourself go 10 percent below it. Just concentrate on moderate, sustainable improvement."[1] In the estimation of the Lakers coaching staff, a one percent improvement in five areas for twelve players gave the team a 60 percent aggregate improvement. It paid off, as the Los Angeles Lakers became that year's NBA champions.

The same philosophy Riley incorporated to win basketball titles has been instilled in the leadership at First Assembly. Every year the staff is challenged to improve over the previous year. Over time these small improvements have resulted in significant gains for the church. Every church can make improvements from the year before. Even if a church is experiencing a numerical growth plateau, a pastor can find five areas of the church that can be improved over the former year.

The prayer ministry can become a little more effective, the church office can become a little more organized, or the church facilities can become a little more attractive. Seldom is a church's effectiveness and excellence radically changed in a single year, but over time, with slight and constant improvement, the church becomes far more than before. Constant and consistent God-honoring improvement is the key to long-term growth and effectiveness.

Key Twenty-Four
Break Through Barriers with Prayer and Fasting

By the spring of 1999, for the first time during my tenure, First Assembly was experiencing a leveling off in our ministries. We had hit a plateau with our attendance and financial numbers showing a slight decline from the previous year. Even more noticeable was the decline in excitement and enthusiasm. It seemed like a dry and stagnate season. I knew it wasn't God's will and I knew if it persisted, the momentum the church had enjoyed the previous eight years could be stopped and the destiny God had for First Assembly might not be realized.

It appeared that many of our people had allowed complacency in their lives, and our church body needed a spiritual breakthrough. I thought of Isaiah 58:6, "Is this not the fast that I have chosen: / To loose the bonds of wickedness, / To undo the heavy burdens, / To let the oppressed go free, / And that you break every yoke?" As I prayed concerning our church situation, I sensed that the Lord was calling us to a time of repentance and consecration through fasting and prayer.

As the senior pastor, I sensed the Lord leading me on a forty-day fast. Though there is a time to fast in secret, (Matt. 6:16-18), there is also a time to fast publicly (Jonah 3:5, Ezra 8:21, and Joel 2:15). This was a public fast, and I announced my intention of fasting forty days. I called on the rest of our church body to participate in some way. A few people joined me for the whole forty days, or for a good portion of the time. Many church members fasted one day a week, some fasted one meal a day, and others fasted processed sugars; but nearly everyone did something. In addition, I asked everyone to fast secular media during the forty-day period. When it was over, many said fasting media was the most significant thing they did during the forty days. During this time we had the church open for prayer throughout the day. We also had a week of nightly worship, prayer, testimonies, a short message, and repentance.

When the forty days were over, it was as if we had a new church. The excitement, vibrancy, and momentum were back. We saw a sudden and dramatic increase in our attendance and finances. When we took God seriously, turning to Him in fasting and prayer, we saw a great breakthrough. There are many methods, principles, and strategies of church growth, but ultimately it is God who builds the church. Times of fasting and prayer demonstrate our serious dependence upon Him, change our hearts, and bring God's blessing.

Key Twenty-Five
Stay Long Enough to Make a Difference

It has been said that most pastors reach their highest levels of effectiveness after their fifth year at a church. If you are being the leader God has called you to be, the longer you stay the more trust and confidence you are able to build in your congregation. Pastoral effectiveness is difficult to determine in the short run. If we had left First Assembly after four years, our impact on our church and on our community would have been minimal. The impact we've made seems to have been exponential, as each year builds on the former year.

Each of the most influential churches in our nation were at one time led by a pastor who served a long tenure. As a general rule, I believe pastors who regularly move to a new church every few years are detrimental to Kingdom purposes. I know there are times when things may not work out in a certain location. But too often pastors leave over a little adversity that they should have ridden out or because another offer looks more attractive. I'm not saying pastors need to spend their entire ministry life in one location, but if God has called them to a location, they need to stay long enough to make a difference.

Your church can make a difference in its community and in its world for Jesus Christ. I hope this book has provided some inspiration and insight to assist you in that purpose. We have a mighty God who is ready, willing, and more than able to accomplish great things in your city. May the world see the glory and greatness of this big God in your city.

Todd Hudnall's Personal
Core Life Values

1. God's Word is the basis of my faith and conduct. As such, I must listen to it, read it, study it, memorize it, meditate in it, and live it.
2. My personal relationship with God is the most important aspect of my life. As such, prayer must be a daily priority.
3. Life is to be lived in abiding dependence upon God and in humble service before men.
4. I have been made in the image of God and redeemed by the blood of Jesus. As such, in Christ I am completely forgiven, totally accepted, deeply loved, and fully pleasing to God. I must see others and myself in light of this truth.
5. I must live a life of authenticity. I want to be the unique person God created me to be.
6. I must be continually growing and allowing Christ to be more fully formed in me.
7. Holiness, integrity, and character are essential to a great life.
8. Life must be viewed in light of eternity and the imminent return of Jesus Christ.
9. I will be held accountable for my life and must steward it faithfully.
10. Lost people are important to God and must be important to me.
11. Whatever I sow in life, I will reap. As such, I must choose to do what is difficult and necessary instead of what is easy and unnecessary.

12. I must add value to the lives of those around me. I know I will only succeed by helping others around me succeed.
13. My family takes priority over my profession, education, and recreation. I desire those closest to me to love and respect me the most.
14. My attitude towards life will determine life's attitude towards me.
15. Be a person known for genuine Christian love.

Todd Hudnall's Personal
Mission Statement

To find happiness, fulfillment, and value in living, I, TODD HUDNALL will glorify God in all my life, loving and enjoying Him, becoming more like Him in my character, being a witness of Him, and serving His purpose for my generation.

I will become a whole-hearted **WORSHIPER**, worshiping my God in spirit and in truth, having a passion for His presence, and continually enjoying sweet communion with Him.

I will become a dedicated and fervent **DISCIPLE**, denying myself, taking up my cross, and following Jesus Christ, developing the habits of a disciple, and allowing Christ to be more fully formed in me.

I will become a loving **HUSBAND**, treating my wife with honor and respect, loving her as Christ loves the Church and considering her above myself.

I will become an inspiring visionary **LEADER**, taking people in the direction God is leading, being an example of a Christ-follower, continually growing in my leadership, mentoring other emerging leaders, and becoming the servant of all.

I will become a life-giving **TEACHER**, communicating the whole counsel of God's Word honestly, creatively, and passionately. I will be a life-long learner.

I will become a caring **PASTOR/ EVANGELIST**, always shepherding the small flock under my care. I will reach out to lost and stray sheep, making sure all of God's flock for which I am responsible are tended to. I will follow Christ in being part of His plan of worldwide redemption.

I will become a faithful **STEWARD**, wisely managing my time, finances, gifts and abilities. I will be a steward of my physical body, my mental facilities, my financial possessions, and my ministry calling.

Our First Assembly Core Values

Universal, Non-Negotiable Values

Every person is valued and is the focus of our ministry.

- ❏ Every person is created to glorify God, who alone is worthy of worship.
- ❏ Every person has the right to a presentation of the Gospel at his level of understanding.
- ❏ Every person needs a Biblical moral compass to guide and protect him through life.
- ❏ Every believer has unique gifts to be developed and used to strengthen the church.
- ❏ Every believer has a purpose in advancing the global mission of the Church of Jesus Christ.

Distinct Non-Negotiable Values

We believe in certain values that characterize our ministry.

- ❏ We believe prayer is the most important ministry of the church from which all other ministry is energized.
- ❏ We believe the key dynamic to life in the church is the Holy Spirit; and we desire His fellowship, leadership, anointing, and manifestations.
- ❏ We believe self-giving love is the mark of the believer and loving relationships should permeate every aspect of church life.
- ❏ We believe the church should continually grow by reaching the lost.

❑ We believe every follower of Christ should be continually growing in Christ-like commitment, character, and wholeness.

❑ We believe anointed, Biblical teaching is the catalyst for transformation in individuals' lives and in the church.

❑ We believe our ministry should be culturally relevant, doctrinally pure, and Biblically uncompromising.

❑ We believe life change happens best in small groups.

❑ We believe both individuals and the church will be held responsible to God for the stewardship of their time, gifts, calling, and finances.

❑ We believe excellence honors God and inspires people.

Our First Assembly
Purpose Statement

❏ To be a corporate body in which man may worship God (1 Cor. 12:13, John 4:23).

❏ To be a channel of God's purpose to build a body of saints being perfected in the image of His Son (1 Cor. 12:28, 14:12, and Rom. 8:29).

❏ To be an agency of God for evangelizing the world (Acts 1:8, Matt. 28:19-20, and Mark 16:15-16).

❏ To be a training center for equipping and releasing believers for ministry (Eph. 4:11-16, Rom. 12:4-8).

❏ To be a community of loving, loyal, and committed servants (Heb. 10:25, John 13:34-35).

Our First Assembly
Mission Statement

To be a corporate body in which man may MAGNIFY God (1 Cor. 12:13, John 4:23). To be a channel of God's purpose to build a body of saints into Christ-like MATURITY (1 Cor. 12:28, 14:12, and Rom. 8:29). To be an agency of God with the MISSION of evangelizing the world (Acts 1:8, Matt. 28:19-20, and Mark 16:15-16). To be a training center for equipping and releasing believers for MINISTRY (Eph. 4:11-16, Rom. 12:4-8). To be a community of loving, loyal, and committed MEMBERS of God's family (Heb. 10:25, John 13:34-35).

Our First Assembly Vision

It is the dream of a place where people can have an encounter with the living God, where the Holy Spirit is given control, and the Kingdom of God is manifested. Where the hurting, the hopeless, the discouraged, the depressed, the oppressed, and the confused can find love, acceptance, forgiveness, healing, help, hope, guidance, and encouragement.

It is the dream of saturating the Deep East Texas area with the Good News of Jesus Christ through every available means.

It is the dream of thousands of believers growing together into a Biblically functioning community. A place where people of diverse race, age, gender, and socioeconomic standing come to know God and become part of the family of faith. Where, through Biblical instruction, interaction, and application, people develop into committed disciples of Jesus Christ. It is the dream of a fellowship of people worshiping, praying, loving, laughing, learning, sharing, caring, celebrating, and serving together.

It is the dream of training, mentoring, equipping, and sending out hundreds of career missionaries, pastors, and church workers all around the world. It is the dream of mothering and planting churches.

It is the dream of a regional church that profoundly impacts Deep East Texas and the world with the Gospel of the Lord Jesus Christ.

Format adapted from Rick Warren's, *Purpose Driven Church*, (Grand Rapids, Michigan: Zondervan Publishing House, 1995), p. 43.

Our First Assembly Vision Statement

To be an authentic community of believers in Jesus Christ who are impacting Deep East Texas and our world. We're a regional church and a Bible training center where people experience the living God, have their lives transformed by His grace, and are prepared for successful living. We're a church that is multi-generational, racially diverse, and impacts every aspect of our society.

Experiencing God, transforming lives, building people and impacting our world.

We will do so by . . .

. . . providing a place of dynamic, relevant, and anointed worship; by building a body of believers into fully devoted, Spirit-filled, Christ-like disciples; by aggressively reaching out to the unchurched, unsaved, and irreligious; by equipping, training, and releasing an army of saints for the work of the ministry; and by becoming a community of loving, loyal, and caring servants.

Our First Assembly Strategy

1st Priority Is Prayer (Matt. 21:13, James 5:16, 1 Thess. 5:17, and Eph. 6:18)

Authentic Christian Living (2 Tim. I:9, 1 Thess. 4:11-12, 2 Cor. 3:2, and Col. 1:10)

Stewardship (Matt. 25:14-30, Rom. 14:12, and 1 Cor. 4:2)

Small Groups (Acts 5:42, 16:40, 20:20)

Excellence of Ministry (Rom. 16:19, Phil. 4:8, and Num.18:29)

Meaningful Celebration Services (Psalm 122:1, 1 Cor 14:11)

Building Bridges to Reach the Unchurched (2 Cor. 5:18-20, 1 Cor. 9:22, and Rom. 15:7)

Lay Ministry Mobilization (1 Peter 4:10, 1 Cor 12:5, 27, Exod. 18:13-26, Eph. 4:12, Heb. 6:1, and 2 Pet. 3:18)

Yieldedness to the Holy Spirit (Eph. 5:18, Gal. 5:22-25, Rom. 15:19, and 1 Cor. 2:4)

First Assembly of God
Lufkin, Texas

Year—to—Year Statistical Comparison

ATTENDANCE COMPARISON	1991	1992	1993	1994	1995	1996	1997	1998	1999	2000
Sunday Morning Celebration	273	321	373	434	516	673	940	1041	1205	1501
% of Increase	6%	18%	16%	17%	19%	30%	40%	10%	14%	25%
Sunday School(Main Session)	216	230	258	300	354	420	519	565	571	588
Sunday School(Extension)	-	-	-	-	40	80	40	50	50	50
Total in Small Groups (not in Sunday School)	-	-	78	120	185	202	245	280	328	363
Total Average Attendance in Christian Education	-	-	333	360	489	631	822	896	949	1001
Sunday Evening	180	180	190	217	235	306	518	541	526	530
Mid-Week Services	170	175	185	212	310	374	460	480	470	682
Adult Church Voting Members	136	137	148	228	244	329	384	451	542	642
Adherents (Adults & Children)	500	610	670	800	950	1150	1650	1750	2000	2400

First Assembly of God
Lufkin, Texas

Year—to—Year Statistical Comparison

MINISTRY COMPARISON	1991	1992	1993	1994	1995	1996	1997	1998	1999	2000
Conversions	30	100	79	203	391	553	1354	893	990	1199
Baptisms in the Holy Spirit	6	10	7	15	37	86	100	111	105	106
Water Baptism	10	15	14	24	26	107	206	111	128	110
Total Home Groups	-	-	12	14	20	18	28	36	34	32
Total Small Groups	-	-	-	-	-	23	38	45	42	125
New Adult Church Members	11	32	47	59	50	145	117	76	165	125

Endnotes

Chapter 3

[1] Jack Hayford, "Today's Loudest Call," *Ministries Today* (January-February 1999), p. 21.

[2] Kenneth O. Gangel, *Feeding and Leading,* (Wheaton, Illinois: Victor Books, 1989), pp. 30-31.

[3] George Barna, *The Second Coming of the Church,* (Nashville, Tennessee: Word Publishing, 1998), p. 105.

[4] Ken Blanchard, Phil Hodges, and Bill Hybels, *Leadership by the Book,* (Colorado Springs, Colorado: Water Brook Press, 1999), pp. 42-43.

[5] John Maxwell, *Qualities of a Leader,* (Nashville, Tennessee: Thomas Nelson, 1999), p. 133.

[6] Stephen R. Covey, *The Seven Habits of Highly Effective People,* (New York: Simon and Schuster, 1989), p. 95.

[7] Brian Tracy, "The Psychology of Success," (Chicago, Illinois: Nightengale-Conant).

[8] Bob Greene, *Keep the Connection,* (New York: Random House) 1999.

[9] Brian Tracy, "The Psychology of Success," (Chicago, Illinois: Nightengale-Conant).

[10] John Maxwell, "Priorities: The Pathway to Success," (Atlanta, Georgia, Injoy).

[11] Charles Hobbs, "Your Time and Your Life," (Chicago, Illinois: Nightengale-Conant).

[12.] Stephen R. Covey, *The Seven Habits of Highly Effective People,* (New York: Simon and Schuster, 1989), p. 150.

[13.] John Maxwell, "Priorities: The Pathway to Success," (Atlanta, Georgia, Injoy).

[14.] Ibid.

[15.] Kenneth Gangel, *Feeding and Leading,* (Wheaton, Illinois: Victor Books, 1989), p. 75.

[16.] Ibid., p. 78.

[17.] E.M. Bounds, *Power Through Prayer,* (Grand Rapids, Michigan: Baker Book House,1972), p. 5.

[18.] John Maxwell, *Developing the Leader Within You,* (Nashville, Tennessee: Thomas Nelson, 1993), p. 45.

[19.] Richard Foster, *Celebration of Discipline.* (New York: Harper Collins Publishers, 1998), p. 7.

[20.] Brian Tracy, "The Psychology of Success," (Chicago, Illinois: Nightengale-Conant, 1986).

[21.] Ibid.

Chapter 4

[1.] Tommy Barnett, "How to Pray for Vision," (*Enrichment, Winter 2000*), p. 34.

[2.] George Barna, *The Power of Vision,* (Ventura, California: Regal Books, 1992), pp. 12-15.

[3.] Ibid., p. 15.

4. Aubrey Malphurs, *Leadership Handbook of Practical Theology.* (Grand Rapids, Michigan: Baker Books, 1994), p. 159.

5. John Maxwell, *The 21 Irrefutable Laws of Leadership,* (Nashville, Tennessee: Thomas Nelson, 1998), p. 37.

6. Aubrey Malphurs. *Strategic Planning,* (Grand Rapids, Michigan: Baker Books, 1999), p. 79.

7. Ibid., p. 79

8. Ibid., pp. 79, 83.

9. Michael Clarensau, Steven Mills, and Sylvia Lee, *We Build People.* (Springfield, Missouri: Gospel Publishing House, 1998), p. 42.

10. Ibid., p.42

11. Aubrey Malphurs, *Strageic Planning.* (Grand Rapids, Michigan: Baker Books, 1999), p. 100.

12. Rick Warren, *The Purpose Driven Church.* (Grand Rapids, Michigan: Zondervan Publishing House, 1995), p. 96.

13. Ibid., pp. 100-101.

14. Aubrey Malphurs, *Strategic Planning.* (Grand Rapids, Michigan: Baker Books, 1999), p. 156.

15. Elmer Towns, *Evangelism and Church Growth.* (Ventura, California: Regal Books, 1995), p. 348.

16. Rick Warren, *The Purpose Driven Church.* (Grand Rapids, Michigan: Zondervan Publishing House, 1995), pp. 139-152.

17. Ibid., p. 111.

[18] Ibid., p. 130.

Chapter 6
[1] Elmer Town, *Friend Day*, (Elkton, Maryland: Church Growth Institute, 1994) Cassette program.

Chapter 7
[1] Gary McIntosh and Glen Martin, *Finding Them and Keeping Them*, (Nashville, Tennessee: Broadman & Holman Publishers, 1992), p. 10.

[2] Jonathan Gainsbrugh, *Winning the Backdoor War*, (Elk Grove, CA: Harvest Church, 1993), p. 81.

[3] Ibid., p. 92.

[4] Ibid., p. 102.

[5] Ibid., p. 127.

Chapter 10
[1] Pat Riley, *The Winner Within*, (New York, New York: The Berkley Publishing Group, 1993), p. 163.

About the Author

Todd Hudnall is the senior pastor of First Assembly of God in Lufkin, Texas. He is a popular conference speaker on the subjects of leadership, spiritual formation, and church growth. His wife Kelly serves with him in ministry. You can contact him at:

Todd Hudnall
First Assembly of God
P.O. Box 151038
Lufkin, TX 75915

Additional copies of the book may be ordered at:

www.toddhudnall.com

For special pricing on orders of ten books or more, call:

First Assembly of God
(936) 632-3540